MW00479118

NOT MANY
DAYS
FROM NOW

Experiencing Scriptural Truth about
the Baptism of the Holy Spirit

NOT MANY DAYS FROM NOW

Experiencing Scriptural Truth about
the Baptism of the Holy Spirit

DAVID SPEICHER

Endorsement

In this timely treatise, Pastor David Speicher highlights the very heart of Jesus in His sending the Holy Spirit, after His resurrection. The promise, the purpose and the power are made clear and will draw the reader into the Biblical explanation of the Spirit's multi-faceted ministry. From personal experience and years of transforming discipleship, Pastor Speicher takes somewhat mis-understood terminology about the Holy Spirit and makes it personal, useable and, most of all, desirable. I echo the vital question of the Apostle Paul to disciples in Ephesus, "Did you receive the Holy Spirit when you believed?" You'll find the answer to that question (and more) in this book!

Dr. Clem Ferris
Itinerant Prophet/Teacher
Grace Church
Chapel Hill, NC

NOT MANY
DAYS
FROM NOW

© 2021 David Speicher

Cover Design and Interior Layout by Uberwriters Christian Ghostwriters
www.uberwriters.com

ISBN 978-1-7369519-0-3 paperback
ISBN 978-1-7369519-1-0 eBook

Table of Contents

Preface

I have many books in my library besides the Bible, and this may surprise you but I am not in complete agreement with any of them except the Bible. Think of it this way—some books have nuggets and veins of truth in them, while others have their own respective mother lodes. I don't reject the whole book simply because I do not agree with a subject in the book.

That being said, when I wrote *Not Many Days from Now,* I knew I had to include the list of books that have been so challenging and encouraging to me over the past few years. My rationale is to provide some different views of the "mountain" for you. I have therefore compiled a list of nuggets, veins, and mother lodes for you to read on your own and decide for yourself what category you would put them in.

To me these works are a tremendous blessing, and I so appreciate the effort these authors have put into presenting the material. By the way, if an author didn't believe his or her work was tapping into a mother lode, they would not have started the project to begin with, so please remember to be kind to others (and if you haven't gone through the ordeal of writing a book, it might be best to hold your peace until you do).

The list that follows is a collection of wonderful works by others who were further along than me in this all-important mission to discover the truth about the Holy Spirit. I value each of their contributions deeply although I do not make the assumption that these books will have the same impact on you. If, however, these books can help you the way they have helped me, they're worth presenting.

Recommended Reading
1. *The Promise of the Father* by Jeff Canfield[1]

Dr. Canfield is an esteemed professor with Logos University. His stern challenges propelled me to become a better writer, which I am in the process of doing. *The Promise of the Father* is an excellent book that first provoked my thinking regarding the baptism of the Holy Spirit. Dr. Canfield's book took me back to a careful study of John 20 to not only define *what* salvation is but to see *when* it happened. This in turn begged the question, "Exactly what is Jesus saying in Acts 1:4,8?" Although I do not agree with everything in his book, I will be grateful for the rest of my life for the mother lode of truth found within it regarding the baptism of the Holy Spirit.

2. *Fresh Wind, Fresh Fire* by Jim Cymbala[2]

Although this book has been around for a while, it has a timeless quality to it. As the author describes his decision to walk away from church-growth strategies, he is the first author I have read who pursued the presence of God corporately and saw the power of God manifested as a result. Like a salmon swimming upstream, bold enough to move in the opposite direction of so many other fish going with the flow, I was drawn to Jim Cymbala's faith as he described pursuing God's presence in prayer. In our church we have incorporated a common language and modality as a result of this author's writing. We call it our "3 P's": Presence, Power, and Programming. This means we pursue the presence of God first, which leads to the power of God being manifested, which in turn leads to the programming necessary to sustain healthy presence. This book will very likely change your leadership perspectives, especially as it relates to being led by the Holy Spirit.

3. *Your Spiritual Gifts* by Donald Hohensee and Allen Odell[3]
For those who are new to understanding the spiritual gifts and want a fairly broad foundation to build upon, this work is a great nugget. It is not exhaustive but it is very informative and biblically based. It will provide the reader a good starting point for further investigation.

4. *He Still Speaks* by Wayne Drain and Tom Lane[4]
Although this book does not speak specifically to the baptism of the Holy Spirit, it does address the programming a church can have after the culture of the five-fold ministry is established. This work is wonderfully constructed, especially regarding how to establish healthy balance and boundaries in ministry life. For those who are looking to transition into a Holy-Spirit-filled Church, this book contains outstanding nuggets and veins of practicality.

5. *Culture of Honor* by Danny Silk[5]
A remarkable book with an explanation of the integral nature of honor in the functioning of the Church. The examples you find in this book are a perfect picture of the mechanics of honor and love as they should be intentionally pursued in relationship with others. Honor is one of the key components in pursuing the presence of God, and this author does an exceptional job of practically valuing honor so you can

see and contrast your normal mode of operation with his examples. He is on point with the title too—the way to sustain a supernatural environment is through honoring the Father, Son, and Holy Spirit, and honoring all human relationships too.

6. *Understanding the Fivefold Ministry* by Matthew D. Green[6]
What I find beneficial about this work is the conglomeration of viewpoints offered. There are a wide range of powerful authors who collaborate, enabling you, at the very least, to spring-board from this book and launch into other great material as you find authors with viewpoints that resonate with you. This is an excellent book for anyone wanting to understand more about the fivefold ministry.

7. *Crossing Over: Getting to the Best Life Yet* by Paul Scanlon[7]
This book is the mother lode. If there is ever going to be a fresh step for you in how you perceive the ministry of the Church, there is no doubt in my mind this book will be an impetus for that transition. This profound work is the simple story of a man who pastored a church and had the courage to change. My desire for you is change, specifically in your development as a Holy-Spirit-filled follower of Jesus Christ.

8. *Relational Transformation* by Mark Tubbs[8]
Mark Tubbs is a modern-day apostle. His journey into the depths of truly honoring the Holy Spirit by recognizing the value and importance of God's leadership through the Holy Spirit in the modern Church is something all of us should take note of. What followed Mark's submission to the Holy Spirit (not only in the direction of his life, but also in the words that God chose to describe the functioning of the Church) was explosive, God-constructed, building. This work is important and very informative in the functioning

of the Church, and is a must read for those who desire to see the practical mechanics of a five-fold ministry. Although this author focuses on the ministry of the apostle, his secondary messages go into weighty detail regarding the other five-fold gifts.

All of these titles and others have had significant influence on *Not Many Days from Now*. I desire to honor as many as I can remember of those whom I have read, heard, and studied. Thank you to all of you—your contributions are appreciated. This work is truly built on the shoulders of giants.

Introduction

In school I was taught that unless you desire to be entertained, look for the premise of the book early on so you can see if the author conveys what he or she said they would. In light of this I would like to state the premise for this book up front: primarily I want you, the reader, to grasp and fully understand how crucial it is to be *filled* with the Holy Spirit. I want you to know the biblical foundation, or maybe better said, the theological praxis for the filling of the Holy Spirit, and that the filling is very likely more than you think. I want you to see how important it is that you go further with the Holy Spirit than where you are, and that you do this because you want to, not because you have to. I wish to share my personal introduction to the Holy Spirit, and how I have found biblical spiritual power in life by giving more room in me to the Holy Spirit so He can accomplish His will in and through me.

Just so you gain a better understanding of me, and to provide some context for your short reading journey, I have a Doctorate of Ministry in Applied Theology, a Doctorate of Philosophy in Systematic Theology, and a Master's Degree in Counseling. I feel too educated for anyone's good, but perhaps this will give you a better sense of why I think or say certain things the way I do.

In all sincerity, I am overjoyed to have the privilege of sharing what I have learned with you, and I'm humbled and honored you would consider reading this work. I don't deserve the privilege and am certainly not entitled to it, but I am compelled to be obedient to God, and whatever good comes to you from reading this book (hopefully it is a lot), it is a testimony to what the Holy Spirit has done in my life. I am eternally grateful for the patience and understanding of God, because it took me many years to incorporate what the Holy Spirit showed me. Armed with this knowledge, however, I believe it will take you a lot less time.

If I may offer some encouragement before we start, please read slowly and consider carefully what you are reading, and especially pay attention when the Holy Spirit prompts you to think about the content in the context of your life and ministry. What I'm saying is when you find yourself thinking, *What would this look like in my life or ministry?* the Holy Spirit is prompting a discussion with you!

Please allow me to pray for you: "Lord, bless this sweet reader—give them wisdom and understanding as they embrace our great Helper in a fresh and wonderful way, with joy and eagerness. In Jesus' name I ask. Amen."

One more thing, if you are looking for a formula to receive the Holy Spirit, you won't find one. If you are looking for techniques to expedite the process of being filled, you won't find those either. The key word is... wait for it... *need*. Do you *need* the Holy Spirit? When you decided to become a Christian you did so because you acknowledged your need for the Savior. Need prompted you to move. The filling of the Holy

Do you need the Holy Spirit?

Spirit is *exactly* the same. If you do not understand our desperate need for the Holy Spirit, forget it. There is not one saved person on Earth who didn't first recognize the need for Jesus in his or her life. Likewise, there is not one Holy-Spirit-baptized person on Earth who didn't feel the need to be baptized. Think about that.

Rationale for Topic

You are getting ready for a journey as you hold this book in your hand. So, it is only fair that I tell you why I wrote the book in the first place. I have several reasons and I will keep them short. After all, who wants to stay at the beginning of anything for very long, especially an exciting journey?

Several relevant and simple questions have to be answered to lay a foundation for why you would continue reading:

1. Why Did I Write the Book?

I've actually answered this question in the first paragraph, but I will reiterate with one distinction—*evangelism.* I want to bring to your attention how crucial it is to be *filled* with the Holy Spirit so you can fulfill your part in the Great Commission (Matthew 28:16-20). I want you to know the biblical foundation—the theological praxis—for the filling of the Holy Spirit, and that the filling is very likely more than you think.

This Bible-based process will infinitely enrich your relationship with God, and subsequently your life, but the ultimate goal is *evangelism.* I want you to see how important it is that you go further with the Holy Spirit than where you are, and that you do this because you want to, not because you have to. Again, the ultimate end is to stop trying to fulfill the Great Commission in your own power, and submit to the

Holy Spirit to enable you to rescue others.

It is as simple as that, yet vastly profound because the work of the Holy Spirit means so much more for *your* personal life and ministry. The degree to which you receive what I am communicating, and apply it to your life, is the degree to which the Holy Spirit can reveal your potential to you. Which leads me to the next question...

2. Who Should Read the Book?

I wrote this book with the lay-reader in mind, carefully avoiding theologically pretentious language so anyone can grasp the concepts. Don't let that detract from the depth of the material. If, however, I was forced to narrow my target audience down to a single group it would be young ministry leaders, or any person interested in the Holy Spirit, but who might be afraid due to hearing "that stuff is of the devil." This book is for anyone who feels God's prompting towards the deeper life in His Spirit, but they just aren't sure of the doctrinal soundness of pursuing the baptism in the Holy Spirit. Basically this book is for anyone locked up in the prison of religion; anyone taught the Holy Spirit is "there" but for all intents and purposes, He is barely able to be active in their life.

3. What Is the Premise behind the Book?

There is a very clear algorithm for New Covenant ministry in the book of Acts; a crystal-clear method. In short, the Holy Spirit fell and the early Church did the acts. In the modern, western Church, however, young pastors pursue the mega-church model instead. They hope that submitting to novel programming they'll find the power of God. They have it backwards—it is the *presence* of God that brings the power of God. As you'll clearly see, the Holy Spirit was sent to

Earth by our Lord Jesus and *He* brings the power.

In the next section I will expound on all three points in a practical way, but please bear in mind the aptly titled urgency of topic:

Urgency of Topic

I don't have many complaints, but chief among them is what is going on in the world around us. What catches my attention isn't all the sin in the world, it's the inability of the Church to do much about it in our present structure and condition. We are attempting to continue on as we always have, doing our normal church thing. The world seems to be getting worse and worse while we develop church-excellence strategies. These strategies are good, but insufficient because they add to the internal focus. We are becoming more fixated on what is happening inside the church walls than what is happening outside. Our focus has been reduced to a question that has stymied our missional mindset: "I wonder what I am going to get from the service today?" With our spiritual egocentricism we have built a wall between a lost world and the Church.

By sending the Holy Spirit in power to baptize, Jesus empowered the Church to reach the lost. The Church is meant to be sent into the world full of the Holy Spirit, but we have only half the equation and half the ingredients, yet we wonder why we have no power. What we have in the Church currently is evangelism in one hand and the Holy Spirit doctrine in another. Suppose I wanted chocolate milk and I held milk in one hand and

How do you think the church as a whole is doing with evangelism in our era?

chocolate in the other, do I have chocolate milk? We are all about the sending, but what preceded that in the book of Acts was the baptism of the Holy Spirit.

How do you think the church as a whole is doing with evangelism in our era? Yeah, I feel the same way. It seems in our day we have a lot going on inside the walls of the church, but nothing outside the walls. If we look at the book of Acts we see there was a balance between what was happening inside and outside the walls of the church. The Church had one foot out in the world and one foot in the believers' gatherings. They were stable and balanced.

In our day there seems to be a lot of teaching on how to maintain a church, how to have the best of everything in a church, who should do what, how to do it and why, so that our particular church and it's programs grow. I think we can conclude that in our era we can be very "inside-the-walls focused" (online walls too). Pointing fingers is not relevant, yet an accurate diagnosis of the problem has to happen or we will continue on in the throes of the problem. The problem we have is the world keeps getting worse and worse and the churches seem to keep getting better and better... How can this be possible?

I believe the root of the problem is we have shut the door on the Holy Spirit. We are okay with a little of the Holy Spirit from time to time. We are okay to have a personal experience with the Holy Spirit in our devotions. We certainly want to hear how He is manifesting in revival in other places, but I believe we are afraid of what will happen to our congregations if the Holy Spirit came to us in power. Who would maintain control if He was allowed to move? According to some experts the manifestation of the Holy

Spirit is not a good church growth practice, either.

The Bible, however, testifies that the manifestation of the Holy Spirit outside the walls of the church is precisely what *does* change the world. As a matter of fact, look at the direction Jesus gives to the disciples concerning what was about to happen and why it was going to happen. He gives the disciples the *purpose* for the baptism in the Holy Spirit.

No matter where you are with the concept of being baptized in the Holy Spirit, lay that to the side for a moment. Now look around and consider whether our plan for evangelism is working across denominations, around the world? I think you would agree it is *not*. We evidently need to ask ourselves why.

Let's go to the words Jesus spoke in Acts 1:8: "But you will receive power when the Holy Spirit has come upon you, and you will be my witnesses in Jerusalem and in all Judea and Samaria, and to the end of the earth." Do you see the Holy Spirit power of Acts 1 sweeping the Earth today as it did in the early days of the Church? What is the difference between them and the Church today? Today we use church growth models, which isn't a bad thing at all, but perhaps the programming models should follow the power of God, and the power of God should follow the presence of God. This is vitally important to understand, so let me explain it.

Much of what I see and experience from a church philosophy perspective seems to suggest that if you do your church programming correctly and your church is growing, then the power of God is manifested in your church by a set of measurable success indicators. This isn't wrong, it is simply incomplete if this is how you define winning people for Jesus. Is success in ministry defined by the breadth of ministry created? What we find in the early Church is they pursued the presence of God. Jesus said, "Wait for the Holy Spirit." What followed was the power of God manifested, and *then* the programming was applied so that the manifested presence and power was sustained. But the Holy Spirit led the charge.

You may say, "But we *have* the Holy Spirit, it's no longer time to wait, it's go time!" This may be true in some cases but generally speaking, church programs are currently taking precedence over the true power of Spirit-filled evangelism. I know this because in the book of Acts Jesus shares the motivation and vision of the Holy Spirit, and it is clearly evangelism beyond the walls of the church, *empowered* by the Holy Spirit. Until we have received His power we would do better to wait upon the Lord.

Consider this as well, that not all, but most ministries today act more like vacuum cleaners than fans. In many of the churches I visit I hear the high-pitched sucking sound as they attempt to draw people in numbers. We need all our pastors—every single one has been gifted by the Lord for this time. There are so many good pastors spread throughout the world, yet pastors are not going to change the world—congregations are. Church leaders have spent a lot of time controlling and shaping ministry for the purpose of growth and excellence, and it seems to make sense. The problem is we have hundreds of people staring at the pastor during the weekend service, like he is some kind of professional, hoping they can muster the courage to invite a friend to church someday. They hope if that friend is invited to church and they do show up, they will hear the pastor talk about

Jesus and raise their hand for the altar call.

In contrast, what if it is the baptism by the Holy Spirit, which Jesus said to wait for in Acts 1, will fill a congregation with boldness beyond the greatest of appeals and inspiration by the best of pastors? Would you be at all willing to at least investigate what Jesus said as potentially the most primary need for our day? I am blessed sometimes to see ministries sending people out with the gospel in a beautiful New Testament way. When in the presence of God, you will see the power of God manifested to send people, not to stockpile them. Of course it is to be taken into consideration that there are seasons of growth and seasons of sending that ministries experience.

The early Church was Christ-focused and Holy Spirit-led. My concern is we are currently people-led and people-focused. We are more concerned with not upsetting those who are tithing— who may experience weird or unexplainable spiritual phenomena— than we are with ensuring the presence of the Holy Spirit. With

My concern is we are currently people-led and people-focused.

all the good intent of maintaining a healthy church, the focus on the presence of God seems to have slipped away.

Fear not, though, what this book aims to do is to highlight the importance of bringing the presence of God back into our churches. Let's study scripture to realign with the New Testament Power that will change the world as He did in the early days of the Church.

There is another urgent matter this book will address.

What if you found out you could "level up" so to speak?

What if there was a greater amount of power available to you so you could rise up to be and do more than you can imagine for the Kingdom of God? Prior to being baptized in the Holy Spirit I had conclusions that were just plain misguided. In this book I have confronted some of the *misguided notions* often associated with the baptism of the Holy Spirit. The following are some examples:

- I have already received all the expression of the Holy Spirit I will ever get when I was saved.

- The Holy Spirit does not work that way anymore.

- Holy-Spirit-filled people are cuckoo for Cocoa Puffs.

- Holy-Spirit-filled people flow through life only on emotion and miss the deeper things of God.

- The Bible doesn't teach that I should or even need to be filled with the Holy Spirit.

- Look at all that has been accomplished by people who have not been filled with the Holy Spirit.

I want to address these misconceptions in love by looking closely at what the Bible teaches us, and give you a safe place to explore what the Bible says. I would like you to really listen to what the Bible teaches about the baptism of the Holy Spirit. Make no mistake, this is urgent! Your interpretation of scripture is critical here. I have often found our interpretation of scripture is precisely where the devil deals a deathblow to life and ministry.

Do you believe the Holy Spirit is the one who gave you your interpretation? Do you really? Or do you believe your interpretation is a box enabling you to understand Him? What if I told you your box of understanding and interpretation is too small? Way too small. There is no way to box the Holy Spirit in anything or in any way. Name a box He has been put into and I will show you how He shatters that box every time. The Holy Spirit cannot and will not be contained. Guess what… your theology is one of the worst boxes into which you could ever try to place Him. This is really great news, because you're about to experience the greatest freedom and empowerment of your life. *If you allow the Holy Spirit to guide you through this process.*

I suggest this to start: recognize the Holy Spirit wants to reveal to you who He is according to the Bible, and that you aren't even close to understanding who He is. If Jesus has sent the Holy Spirit as the Helper and Guide, would it make sense for you to understand more about Him? Maybe you could even say, "I need more understanding from You Holy Spirit."

You see, when we say to ourselves (which ultimately we are saying to God), "I have enough and I know enough of You," we have put God in a box, along with the power He desires to put into us for completing our life mission. Take the step of faith and open your heart to seek more. I know you feel it… the sense that there is much, much more.

✳✳✳

Personal Prayer
Lord, this is somewhat scary, but I am comfortable saying I need You. If I have put You in a box and you want to show me more, I am willing. Lord, I only know what I have been taught—I submit even that to You right now. In the mighty name of Jesus.

Salvation
Chapter One

———⊰※⊱———

I have been known to say every series I preach is the most important series in the world. That's just how I roll; when God speaks to my heart through His Word, the desire to make that Word known to others is paramount. What we're going to discover in this book, though, really *is* the most important lesson in the entire world. It's why I decided to write this book. The unlimited power of the Holy Spirit is a part of God that will change this world. He's here on Earth with us, and even more importantly, He's in us! In this chapter we will be delving into nothing short of how we can access the power of God's Holy Spirit.

———⊰※⊱———

One distinctive characteristic of the Holy Spirit is He cannot be contained.

This is truly the most important message for the New Testament Church.

Peoples' perception of the Holy Spirit falls into a broad continuum. On one end of the spectrum, people think you're weird and freaky if you delve into the Holy Spirit's gifts and power—they believe your spiritual walk is going to get all wonky, really fast. On the other end of the continuum, people are focused *only* on the presence of the Holy Spirit, crying, "I just want more and more of the Holy Spirit's power," often ignoring the Word of God. All of us fall somewhere along the length and breadth of this continuum, and yet there is still a balanced approach to the work of the Holy Spirit in our current day. My aim is to "de-weird" the Holy Spirit for the entire body of Christ. My hope is the Church will fully move into a place where all of us will be open to the Holy Spirit.

I'll give you the bottom line up front, though: if you do a scripture study, one distinctive characteristic you'll always find concerning the Holy Spirit is *He cannot be contained.* There is just no way we can control Him. When the Holy Spirit is invited to move in a church, He *will* break out beyond that church. Once He is accepted by, and dwells within a person, He *will* break out through that person to help others know Jesus. When He bathes a nation with His presence, He *will* strive to touch the surrounding nations. There is no container on this Earth that can hold the Holy Spirit.

If You Have Ears to Hear
We generally struggle with things we don't understand, but there is one crucial aspect you must recognize concerning the Holy Spirit: you will *never* fully understand Him—at least not while you walk this Earth. You may think you understand Him, then He'll do something in your life and you'll think, *Oh my goodness… what was that?*

And if you have ears to hear, you'll hear Him say, "That was Me."

People want things in their proper place (as they perceive them to be proper). We want everything to be controlled and predictable, yet the desire to contain and control does not describe the Holy Spirit. The Holy Spirit is 100% God, and He chooses to express His Godliness through you and me—through our bodies, souls, and spirits. As we embark upon this journey to better understand the Holy Spirit and His work through us, we face a huge question—what will happen along the way?

In truth, I don't know. What I do know is I have been called to deliver a theological praxis—a teaching on the Holy Spirit—through which I hope you will learn to practice, embody, and enact the lessons contained within these pages, especially since I will use scripture to show the validity of what I'm saying. I plan to lay a theological foundation from God's Word that I believe is irrefutable, and it revolves around the *necessity* of the Holy Spirit—how absolutely vital He is to the fulfillment of God's work on Earth.

It's All about Love

To understand the Holy Spirit we must begin with a look at our *salvation.* You might think that doesn't make sense. Why would we be looking at salvation if we're really going to talk about the Holy Spirit?

When I refer to salvation, I'm not simply talking about what we *think* we understand about salvation, but rather what the scriptural term really means. *Everything* about Jesus is a big deal. Did you know that when Jesus says something, it's important? It goes beyond simply what Jesus says; *when* He says something is also a big deal. I'm talking about the *timing* of His words.

3

Let's answer the question: "*When* is salvation?" You may have never thought about this, but in understanding the role of the Holy Spirit in our world today—or the baptism of the Holy Spirit—it is important to recognize these concepts are both keyed in on *when* salvation happens. As we explore the working of the Holy Spirit, my prayer is for God to activate your discernment, that you may recognize His truth.

> *Let's answer the question: "When is salvation?"*

There has been so much profiteering regarding the Holy Spirit, with charlatans claiming many untrue things about Him. My prayer is that we do it right, so we may learn from scripture how to walk in the power of the Holy Spirit. It is absolutely crucial the Church learns about Him today, and we need to learn fast.

Why do we need to learn fast? Time is running out for us to make an impact on this world, and the only way we'll fully do that is by understanding how much the Holy Spirit loves us. When my family and I visit my parents, who are more or less in their ninth decade, their desire is centered on love— they genuinely just want to know how we all are: "What's going on in your life? How are the kids? What's happening at work? How's the church?" At every turn they're looking to bless, to love, to minister… simply because of the love that fills them.

My aim is for you to recognize that the Holy Spirit feels the same way about you, only more so, because the love He has for us is just so radically superior to how any human could ever love. His involvement in your life is based entirely upon love; it's not based upon what you do right and what you do wrong. It's based upon His desire for you to be blessed, to have fellowship with the Father, to deeply know who Jesus is, and to understand the power He's given you. His desire is for you to use the gifts He's given to you, and to eagerly grasp the life and the destiny He's given you.

1 John 3:1 tells us, "See what kind of love the Father has given to us, that we should be called children of God; and so we are. The reason why the world does not know us is that it did not know him." The Holy Spirit is present in John as he writes, prompting the thoughts and feelings that cause John to marvel at God's love. And so it is with *you;* that's why we must dig in to gain a deeper understanding of the place and time of salvation.

As we begin to understand the Holy Spirit, I want you to recognize that your interaction with Him is profoundly relational. His effectiveness in our lives is about how deeply we are connected to Him. Bear in mind as we move forward that God wants to take care of you, and He really wants to be involved in your life. This is why He sent the Holy Spirit, referred to throughout scripture as the Comforter, the Teacher, the Guide, and the Helper.

A key shift in the lives of the disciples is their transition from being Old Testament saints to becoming New Testament saints.

Let's start by having a look at a key shift in the lives of the disciples—their transition from being Old Testament saints to becoming New Testament saints. Old Testament saints followed the Old Testament Law, and by following the Law to the best of their ability and conscience, people became saints of God and were saved.

When the Law was broken a sacrifice was offered—either an animal or herb, whatever the circumstance required. It was all based on the Law—follow the Law and pay penance when you break the Law. We know the disciples were not Law breakers, but rather Law followers. Even though the disciples were contemporaries of Jesus, they were bound to follow the Old Testament Law for their salvation. At the resurrection of Jesus from the dead, the new covenant is established. The old covenant Law was established through Moses in the first five books of the Bible, referred to as the Pentateuch. An example of this can be found in a quick study of the Ten Commandments (Exodus 20). There you will see the Law was given by God through Moses. Verse 22 lists the requirements the Lord gave to the people of Israel for building the altar on which they would make their sacrifices and offerings as a necessity for maintaining peace with God.

With this in mind, there are two passages I would like us to look at briefly. The first is Hebrews 9:21-22:

> "[21] And in the same way he sprinkled with the blood both the tent and all the vessels used in worship. [22] Indeed, under the law almost everything is purified with blood, and without the shedding of blood there is no forgiveness of sins."

When sins were committed, blood was required. This was the old covenant way. I am very glad we exist in a different way with God today—a new covenant. Jesus' blood was required once, for all, for us to live free of this ongoing payment for sin (Hebrews 10:10).

The second passage I want to share with you sings the mechanics of the new covenant. Listen to this:

> [13] And you, who were dead in your trespasses and the

6

uncircumcision of your flesh, God made alive together with him, having forgiven us all our trespasses, [14] by canceling the record of debt that stood against us with its legal demands. This he set aside, nailing it to the cross. Colossians 2:13-14

The disciples were headed toward the new covenant but had not yet attained it. They offered sacrifices, and were considered saints according to the Old Testament Law. Yet, somewhere along the way they transitioned from being Old Testament saints to New Testament, or new covenant saints.

I used to believe that when the Holy Spirit fell upon the first church at Pentecost is when salvation by faith in Jesus Christ was established, but I currently hold a different view. In this book, I will explain how I came to change my perspective, and which scriptures led me to this decision. It all starts with believing Jesus died on the cross, becoming the ultimate sacrifice, fulfilling the Old Testament Law.

When you believe Jesus Christ died on the cross for your sins, you are saved—you're redeemed. Your salvation is not dependent on you following the Old Testament Law, because the new covenant—the New Testament, the Law of love, grace, and mercy—supersedes the Old Testament Law. The question is, "When did that happen for the disciples?" As you will see, it did not happen at Pentecost, but let's turn to God's Word for clarity.

In John's gospel there's a clear statement of unbelief revealed in the text, concerning one of the two disciples who were on their way to Jesus' tomb: "[8] Then the other disciple, who had reached the tomb first, also went in, and he saw and believed; [9] for as yet they did not understand the scripture, that he must rise from the dead" (John 20:8-9).

7

To fully appreciate the deeper nuances of this passage, it's important to understand that a key component—a key tenet of our salvation—is the fact that Jesus rose from the dead, thereby securing salvation for all of us. If He didn't rise from the dead, He would not have defeated the grave, and sin. Jesus *had* to rise from the dead, and in so doing He secured our salvation. The disciples had not experienced this—they had not as-of-yet seen the risen Christ. How could they possibly believe in Christ Jesus as the One who forgives sin and redeems through His blood, if His crucifixion hadn't even happened yet?

> *They had not as-of-yet seen the risen Christ.*

We know the disciples were saved, but they were saved based upon the old covenant. The old covenant was only abolished when Jesus cried out with a loud voice and yielded up His spirit—the precise and symbolic moment the veil in the temple was torn (Matthew 27:50-51). This was the point when the old system was brought to an end. We can infer from scripture that the disciples were saved due to an answer one of them gave to Jesus, when He asked a specific question:

> [15] He said to them, "But who do you say that I am?" [16] Simon Peter replied, "You are the Christ, the Son of the living God." [17] And Jesus answered him, "Blessed are you, Simon Bar-Jonah! For flesh and blood has not revealed this to you, but my Father who is in heaven." Matthew 16:15-17

Here we see Jesus blessed Peter for grasping this revelation, but Peter was blessed under the Old Testament Law, as an Old Testament saint. Even at that point in time, though, and despite Peter knowing Jesus truly is the Messiah, his salvation through grace was not secured because Jesus had not died yet.

Does it change the construct of salvation, knowing the disciples were in between the Old Testament and New Testament definitions of salvation? Does it make a difference that Old Testament salvation was being transitioned into the form it takes in the New Testament? No. It doesn't change the construct of salvation at all.

Essentially, the disciples were not aware of the finished work of Jesus on the cross, because Jesus had not yet gone to the cross to finish it. We who have the clarity of hindsight know exactly when the work on the cross was finished because Jesus clearly stated, while hanging on the cross, "It is finished" (John 19:30b).

Knowing this, the same question kept churning in my mind: "When did post-cross salvation happen? When did the disciples transition from being Old Testament saints to New Testament saints?" Let's keep digging into scripture to find the answer.

The Second Baptism

S o we know the disciples were between the Old Testament and New Testament definitions of salvation, and we know this doesn't change the importance or reality of salvation at all. The question, however, remains, "When did post-cross salvation first take place?"

In John's gospel, Jesus visited the disciples on the day of His resurrection; He breathed on them and told them to receive the Holy Spirit,

> "[21] Jesus said to them again, 'Peace be with you. As the Father has sent me, even so I am sending you.' [22] And when he had said this, he breathed on them and said to them, 'Receive the Holy Spirit'" (John 20:21-22).

Notice in the scripture above, there is nothing in the disciple's response to indicate they said, "No thank you," or "I'm not sure about that." They gladly received what Jesus offered them.

I want to validate the Old Testament salvation of the disciples by looking at the timeline. I find it interesting that in John chapter 20, both Mary Magdalene and the disciples are shown to be in conversation with Jesus. Mary is a very important piece of this puzzle: "Now on the first day of the week Mary Magdalene came to the tomb early, while it was still dark, and saw that the stone had been taken away from the tomb" (John 20:1).

The conversation between Mary and Jesus takes place before Jesus addressed the disciples later in the day. Here's what He said to Mary when He saw her at the empty tomb:

> Jesus said to her, "Do not cling to me, (or do not touch me) for I have not yet ascended to the Father; but go to my brothers (He's talking about the disciples) and say to them, 'I am ascending to my Father and your Father, to my God and your God.'" John 20:17—parentheses mine

So Jesus told Mary He was about to ascend to the Father, and that she should tell His disciples what He had said. Take note of what happens in verse 19—this is very interesting, as it puts the timeline into perspective: "*On the evening of that day*, the first day of the week, the doors being locked where the disciples were for fear of the Jews, Jesus came and stood among them and said to them, 'Peace be with you'" (John 20:19—emphasis mine).

Early in the morning Jesus told Mary Magdalene He was going to ascend to the Father, and then on the evening of that same day He visited the disciples. My question is, what was Jesus doing all day? I believe His statement to Mary speaks for itself—He was about to ascend to His Father, so that is where Jesus was. Well, why in the world would He do that? Another puzzling question is, why couldn't Mary touch

Him? He specifically said, "Don't cling to Me."

Let's work through the verses of scripture that shed light on this issue. We pick up the story where Jesus appeared to His disciples on the evening of that day, the first day of the week:

> [24] Now Thomas, one of the twelve, called the Twin, was not with them when Jesus came. [25] So the other disciples told him, "We have seen the Lord." But he said to them, "Unless I see in his hands the mark of the nails, and place my finger into the mark of the nails, and place my hand into his side, I will never believe." John 20:24-25

Thomas said, "Unless I touch Him, I'm not going to believe." At this point it would be reasonable to consider Thomas' request problematic—Jesus had already said Mary couldn't touch Him. Yet Thomas was ultimately granted his wish:

> [26] Eight days later, his disciples were inside again, and Thomas was with them. Although the doors were locked, Jesus came and stood among them and said, "Peace be with you." [27] Then he said to Thomas, "Put your finger here, and see my hands; and put out your hand, and place it in my side. Do not disbelieve, but believe." [28] Thomas answered him, "My Lord and my God!" John 20:26-28

What happened between the first interaction Jesus had with Mary, after the resurrection, where He said, "Do not touch Me," and the second interaction with Thomas, where He said, "Thomas, give me your hand, put it right into my side"? You have to wonder, *When did this radical change take place?*

I believe Jesus did exactly what He told Mary He was going to do—He ascended to His Father. (I want to credit Dr.

Jeff Canfield, in his book titled *The Promise of the Father,* in which he introduces to the reader in chapter seven, that salvation by grace occurred for the disciples when Jesus breathed on them in the locked room that resurrection night. He summarizes, "Knowing that the Holy Spirit had not yet been sent, the only reasonable explanation for the John 20 upper room experience is the disciples being born again[9].")

If we extrapolate from Revelation chapters 1, 4, and 5, we learn more details about what happened during the time Jesus ascended. In Revelation chapter 5 we're given this picture of the Lion of the tribe of Judah who seems to suddenly transform into the Lamb of God, standing before the throne as though He had been slain (Revelation 5:5-6).

It's a poignant scene that begins with John crying because the heavenly creatures are looking for somebody to take the scroll out of the hand of the Father. John was weeping because no one was found worthy to take the scroll from the Father's hand. The relevant context here is within Greek culture at that time, when a scroll was written, the names of the people who were authorized to open the scroll were written on the outside. In this instance, no one was found worthy to open the scroll, which brought John to tears.

What these images convey to us is that no one was found worthy to open the scroll *until* Jesus ascended and took the scroll from the hand of the Father. He was the Lamb that was slain who became the Lion of the tribe of Judah.

I believe with all my heart that *this heavenly scroll contained the authority to bring redemption to mankind.* I tie my understanding of this to the fact that before Jesus left the Earth for the last time after His resurrection, He told the eleven disciples to go to Galilee, directing them to a specific mountain, where He said to them, "'All authority in heaven and on earth has been given to me'" (Matthew 28:18). I believe that when Jesus took the scroll in Heaven, He had presented Himself to the Father as the perfect Lamb, untouched by anybody, including Mary Magdalene.

Jesus went to the Father to present Himself, and then He came back to Earth to visit the men He loved so much— His disciples whom He had mentored. He showed them the wounds in His hands and side, and allowed them to touch Him. This monumental occasion inaugurated the redemption you and I enjoy today.

Now when Jesus joined His disciples in the locked room on the evening of His resurrection and breathed on them, I believe this was the moment salvation first occurred through faith in Jesus Christ. This moment is where the indwelling Holy Spirit began His work in humanity—not at Pentecost.

Pentecost is marvelous, and we will also explore the details of Pentecost and the Holy Spirit's role there, but imagine what it must have been like for those disciples to see Jesus suddenly appear in a locked room; for Him to come close and breathe His Spirit into them. Imagine their overwhelming wonder at being filled with the Holy Spirit at that point in time, having the Spirit of God indwell them.

> *This was the moment salvation first occurred through faith in Jesus Christ.*

This, of course, raises a question, which serves as a lead-in to the material covered in the rest of this book: "Were the disciples saved through faith in Jesus Christ when Jesus breathed on them?" I believe they were, but together we will examine the scriptures to resolve the matter. Just a few days after this scene took place, Jesus gave His disciples an order:

> ⁴ And while staying with them he ordered them not to depart from Jerusalem, but to wait for the promise of the Father, which, he said, "you heard from me; ⁵ for John baptized with water, but you will be baptized with the Holy Spirit not many days from now." Acts 1:4-5

Jesus knew the disciples were already saved. With great joy in His heart He came back to Earth after having ascended to the Father, and He ministered to these men. They received the Holy Spirit right there, so when Jesus said to them, "Don't run away, don't leave, for not many days from now you will be baptized with the Holy Spirit," if I was one of the disciples I would have said, "There's *more?*"

Two Infillings

In the book of Acts, Jesus explained why a second baptism is necessary. There's a filling, then an additional filling, which is why Jesus said, "But you will receive power when the Holy Spirit has come upon you, and you will be my witnesses in Jerusalem and in all Judea and Samaria, and to the end of the earth" (Acts 1:8).

When a person accepts Jesus Christ as their Savior, the infilling of the Holy Spirit is involuntary. You have no choice in the matter if you accept Jesus as your Lord. It's a part of the salvation process. When you say yes to Jesus, when you accept Him as your Savior, the Spirit of the Lord enters you, and you are sealed by the Holy Spirit. 2 Corinthians 1:21-22 shows this clearly: "²¹ And it is God who establishes us with you in Christ, and has anointed us, ²² and who has also put his seal on us and given us his Spirit in our hearts as a guarantee."

You are marked by the Holy Spirit as a saint of God. This is what happens at salvation, and it's *involuntary*. I want to suggest, however, that the second filling—the "Second Blessing" as some authors have called it—is *completely voluntary*. Jesus calls it the baptism of the Holy Spirit, and this is what we will study through the book of Acts and other scriptures.

When a person accepts Jesus Christ as their Savior, the infilling of the Holy Spirit is involuntary.

From scripture it is clear to see that this second infilling is voluntary—it's your decision—and Jesus even alludes to the purpose behind the Second Blessing: *so we will receive power*. I don't know about you, but I need God's power in my life. Not just so I can be transformed on the inside, but I've come to understand that the hope of the world is Jesus within me and within you. The sad truth is in the Church's present condition, we're not going to get the job done.

The Holy Spirit calls you His temple, or His home. He'll fill you to overflowing, giving you supernatural gifts and abilities. What we do in the body of Christ, though, is we try to contain the Spirit; we try to put Him in a box and say, "Okay, I have an understanding of the Holy Spirit now, so I will sway a little when we sing, and sway when we worship. I'm good with that. *That's* the Holy Spirit!"

Yet, what Jesus says is, "When the Holy Spirit comes upon you, you will have *power* to take My name everywhere." We're worried about containing the Holy Spirit while the

Holy Spirit is primarily concerned about helping us express the love of God in every, and any capacity possible. When a person becomes open and available to the Holy Spirit, that's when the Holy Spirit will fill him or her, but this can happen only once we are open and ready to receive.

When I did reach out to God, desiring to receive the baptism of the Holy Spirit, one of the most visible signs that came about was I became keenly aware of the Holy Spirit's presence in my life. I'll tell you more of my story as we proceed, but briefly, I initially tried to contain the Holy Spirit, and when I took this ignorant course of action I began not only to contain Him, but to squelch Him. Over time, as I gave freedom to the Holy Spirit, He did wonderful things inside of me. The biggest takeaway from my experience of baptism in the Holy Spirit decades ago, was becoming more keenly aware of His presence.

But it was something I had to work at.

Plus, I had to be willing to *keep* working at it because I didn't understand the process, and I kept trying to put a box around Him—bodily, spiritually, and with every aspect of my being. I simply couldn't understand why my experience was being limited, until I stepped into His presence *without trying to limit Him.* This is why scripture tells us plainly and openly, that the anointing of the Holy Spirit abides in you and teaches you (1 John 2:27), but you have to be submitted to the process. You have to want it.

We have considered how the disciples made the transition from salvation under the old covenant into salvation under the new covenant. This is interesting for us to consider but there is a more important question to be asked: do you have a relationship with Jesus? This question is more important because the working of the Holy Spirit doesn't mean anything if Jesus Christ has not saved you from your sin. You cannot have either infilling of the Holy Spirit unless you have submitted to Jesus as your Lord. That's the most important thing you can contemplate right now. Jesus went to Calvary and finished the work of the cross for you. He did it so you could have eternal life; so you would not have to pay the price of your sin throughout eternity. He's intimately aware of your sin, but He took your sin, past, present and future.

Salvation involves understanding that Jesus absolved you of sin. Not only did He die for your sin, He overcame your sin when He rose from the dead. Have you ever asked Jesus to forgive you? Would you be willing to say a prayer? You can ask Him right now, in your present condition. This detail is so important: you will never be able to clean up for Jesus. It's just not possible, and it is not necessary. In your present condition you simply say:

"Jesus, I believe what you did on the cross was for me. You died with my sin. You died because of my sin, and I'm asking you right now to forgive me for sinning, and being a sinner. I receive Your acceptance, Your love, Your forgiveness. Please fill me with your Holy Spirit. Please breathe on me the same way You breathed on Your disciples. I receive the precious gift of the Holy Spirit right now. Jesus, I receive this wonderful blessing from You. I receive hope, and an awareness of Your presence. Thank You, Lord. Thank You for giving salvation to me. Thank You that I am not bound to an old covenant, or to an Old Testament system where I would continually just keep breaking Your laws in the hope that one day redemption would be mine. Thank You for taking Your disciples to the point of believing in Your power to be raised from the dead. Thank You, Lord, for the forgiveness of my sin, and thank you for my new, personal relationship with You—the very Son of God. I give You my life, and I thank You for doing this miracle in me today, and as I continue my journey with You."

My prayer for you, my brothers and sisters, having now accepted Jesus as your Lord and Savior is, "Oh God, please give these precious souls the true and only Holy Spirit, who will bring life, restoration and hope to them. In Jesus name I pray, Amen."

Now that we understand how Jesus saved His disciples and set them apart, we are equipped to answer the question of what the true meaning of Acts 1, verse 4 and verse 8 is. We can study what the unabridged meaning of these scriptures is. The answer will bring us to an understanding of the role the Holy Spirit plays in our lives.

Our ultimate focus as we work through this book, is to reach the moment where you can say, "I just received the Holy Spirit!" We'll go through this process together, and we will see what the Lord does. Strap yourself in for the ride of your life!

The Baptism of the Holy Spirit

Chapter Three

———◁∭▷———

The opening chapter revolved around salvation where we not only looked at what salvation is, but equally as important, *when* did salvation happen? When did salvation under the new covenant start? We concluded salvation first occurred in John 20:22, when Jesus breathed on the disciples in the locked room where they had gathered after His resurrection. He breathed the Holy Spirit out upon them and they received the Holy Spirit. From that point on salvation by faith in Jesus Christ became a reality for humankind.

Jesus came back after ascending to the Father and presented Himself to the disciples; they received salvation because they saw Jesus resurrected, recognizing how wonderful and beautiful this was. Now that we understand how Jesus saved His disciples and set them apart, we are equipped in trying to answer the question of what is the true meaning of Acts 1, verse 4 and verse 5, when Jesus told the disciples they would receive the promise of the Father not many days after (paraphrase of Acts 1:4-5). As mentioned in the previous chapter, the answer to this question will bring us to an understanding of the role the Holy Spirit plays in our lives.

You Will Receive Power

In verse 8, Jesus says, "But you will receive power when the Holy Spirit has come upon you, and you will be my witnesses in Jerusalem and in all Judea and Samaria, and to the end of the earth" (Acts 1:8). Jesus specifically points out they *will receive power* when the Holy Spirit comes upon them. He was talking to the apostles—they're the sent ones—and the plan was for these apostles to spread the Good News of Jesus all over the Earth. Which is exactly what happened. You and I are blessed today, in the name of Jesus, due to the apostolic work of those twelve men. They were filled with power and with the Holy Spirit after they received their salvation about fifty days earlier (in John 20:22). This took place on the evening of Jesus' resurrection, when He walked into the room where they gathered despite the locked doors, because the disciples were fearful of the religious leaders.

Why did Jesus tell them they would receive power when the Holy Spirit came upon them 'not many days' after His ascension?

The question to ask is, "If the disciples were filled with power when they received the Holy Spirit at salvation, why did Jesus tell them they would receive power when the Holy Spirit (the promise of the Father) came upon them 'not many days' after His ascension?"

People refer to the baptism of the Holy Spirit in different

ways, so I prefer to focus on what Jesus said about it during the forty-day period between His resurrection and His ascension:

> [4] And while staying with them he ordered them not to depart from Jerusalem, but to wait for the promise of the Father, which, he said, "you heard from me; [5] for John baptized with water, but you will be baptized with the Holy Spirit not many days from now." Acts 1:4-5

This scripture reveals two aspects of the baptism of the Holy Spirit I want to address: there is a difference between *receiving* the Holy Spirit when you accept Jesus as your savior (scripture is very clear about this), and what happens when you are *filled* with the Holy Spirit when you specifically ask God for this baptism. In this second instance, you have to be ready and hungry to be filled with the Holy Spirit; you must have a strong desire to be filled, and most importantly you must *ask* to be filled.

Before we go into detail on this subject, I want you to understand why it is important for us to dedicate an entire book to process this teaching on the Holy Spirit. The reason is *we all need the Holy Spirit*. I need the Holy Spirit as much as every other believer needs to be filled with the Holy Spirit. Too often I see young ministers hoping that by programming we'll find the power of God. We

———⟨≋⟩———

You may be thinking, *Didn't I receive the Holy Spirit at the point of salvation?*

have it backward. It is the *presence of God* that brings the power of God. The manifest presence of the Holy Spirit brings the power, and in my humble opinion, the Church is in the dark ages regarding knowledge of the work of the Holy Spirit. This is why society is being overrun by evil, and we have such an attrition of young people, especially in cessationist[10] circles. There is simply no power, and the apostle Paul said "the kingdom of God does not consist in talk but in power" (1 Corinthians 4:20).

You may be thinking, *Didn't I receive the Holy Spirit at the point of salvation?*

Yes, you did! Yet there is far more to receiving the full power of the Holy Spirit—being filled—but before we look into this, I'd like to ask a question: "Do you believe the Holy Spirit is God?"

I hope your answer was "Yes," because the Holy Spirit *is* God. He's the third person of the Trinity. He is God, He is Lord. Jesus calls Him our "Helper" with a capital "H," and our "Guide" with a capital "G." He is also called the "Comforter" with a capital "C." This is who the Holy Spirit is.

In Isaiah and the book of Revelation, He is referred to as the sevenfold Spirit of God, and it is He who indwells us. Which brings me to the next question, "Did you know you were shaped by God to be a container?" He knew from the beginning you would be filled with a spirit, so He created you to contain a spirit.

You have the choice to determine what kind of spirit you will be filled with, and what kind of spirit you will be led by. Yet when God handcrafted you and every other human being, He created us to be containers for the Holy Spirit. I'm not saying the Holy Spirit is limited by our spirit—He goes beyond any container into which we try to put Him, but the apostle Paul did say, "But we have this treasure in jars of clay, to show that the surpassing power belongs to God and not to us" (2 Corinthians 4:7). And King David sang, "What is man that you are mindful of him, and the son of man that you care for him?" The Holy Spirit within us is a mind-boggling gift from Heaven.

Now what the enemy attempts to do is to get you filled with a different, inferior spirit; he wants to lead you by a spirit not at all aligned with God. Some people display this as being filled with lust, others with indulgence, while some are filled with pride, and still others with fear. Yes, I am talking about demonization in the unsaved, but even in the case of Christians, our lives can often be led and directed by a spirit that is not the Holy Spirit.

You receive the Holy Spirit at the point of salvation, but that doesn't mean you're led by the Holy Spirit throughout your life. There is something required of you to be aligned with His direction. It's also necessary to understand that whatever container the Holy Spirit is put into, it cannot contain Him—He leaks through every vessel and will not be contained. If you try to contain Him anywhere on Earth, He will spread beyond the Earth. When we invite Him into a city, He will spread beyond that city. If He enters a church, He will go beyond that church. When He is invited into a person He will go beyond the boundaries of that person. Which is the whole point.

When the Spirit of the Lord fills you, He expresses the love of the Father and it's not containable. He flows out through testimony, through love, through our brokenness— He flows out of us and touches the lives of people around us.

While meditating on scripture one day, I began thinking about a light bulb. I was considering how within the Body of Christ, it's normal for us to think about the expression of God to our world through the Church, and how most people look to the pastor as the one initiating God's expression. If the Church was a light bulb most people would consider the pastor to be the filament—the thin metal thread that lights up so the world can see Jesus loves them.

Too often in churches, we feel it's the pastor, the preaching, the ministry, the platform, or the teaching that lights the world. I want to suggest to you that *the pastor is not the filament*—I believe *you are*. I think the pastor is that metal thread at the bottom of the lightbulb, screwed into the power source. The anointing and the power of the Holy Spirit flows into the house through vision, scripture, direction, and authority—yes, these come in through the pastor but he's not the one who lights up the community. You are! Scripture encourages us all to "let your light shine before others, so that they may see your good works and give glory to your Father who is in heaven" (Matthew 5:16).

It's the Holy Spirit who comes in and lights you up so other people can see; this happens *through* the Holy Spirit. The pastor is not the filament of the church, though he definitely is the filament *in his sphere of influence,* just as you are in yours. We are the filament in the places we walk, but it's not a light as strong as when a church body is together and shines corporately with the knowledge of Jesus Christ. Together we're a light to the community, but this only happens as we are filled with the Holy Spirit.

The Holy Spirit is always ready, but so often *we're* not ready. Let me show you a unique picture in the book of Acts:

[1] Now in these days when the disciples were increasing in number, a complaint by the Hellenists arose against

the Hebrews because their widows were being neglected in the daily distribution. ² And the twelve summoned the full number of the disciples and said, "It is not right that we should give up preaching the word of God to serve tables. ³ Therefore, brothers, pick out from among you seven men of good repute, full of the Spirit and of wisdom, whom we will appoint to this duty. Acts 6:1-3

Do you see what's going on here? The apostles are loving on people, they're praying, ministering, laying hands on people, and sharing the Word. Miracles are happening and lives are being transformed, but problems suddenly arise within the local church, which is a very common occurrence.

What the apostles were saying is, "We understand there is a need for greater efficiency in the church. We have to put some programs in place to ensure everybody is cared for, but it feels as if the Holy Spirit does not want this to be our primary focus. Our focus is to minister the Word, so let's raise up people from within the congregation and assign them the duty of serving people at meal times."

Basically, these people were waiters, being raised up to serve the congregation. This was the apostles' way of establishing church staff. The passage continues, saying, "⁴ But we will devote ourselves to prayer and to the ministry of the word.' ⁵ And what they said pleased the whole gathering, and they chose Stephen, a man full of faith and of the Holy Spirit, and Philip..." (Acts 6:4-5a).

Stephen and Phillip were two of the seven servers appointed. This is interesting because Acts chapters 6, 7, and 8 really focus on Stephen and Phillip. What's interesting is these two were raised up by the church to wait tables, but as we keep reading we see this was only one small aspect of their ministry. A few verses later we read: "And Stephen, full of grace and power…"

Where did Stephen get that power? In Acts 1:8 Jesus said, "But you will receive power when the Holy Spirit has come upon you." Stephen received this power at the baptism of the Holy Spirit, and this is how he put God's power to use: "And Stephen, full of grace and power, was doing great wonders and signs among the people" (Acts 6:8).

Today, this would often be perceived as a church problem. Imagine how a modern church leader might respond when seeing how Stephen operated beyond the role appointed to him: "So listen, Stephen, we have a problem. We asked you to step in and lead in a certain area—waiting tables, and serving orphans and widows. That's your job and responsibility. Thank you very much for serving, but now it has come to our attention that you're performing miracles too? We find out people's lives are being transformed… We gave you the responsibility of waiting tables, and now you're doing *our* job. This can't go on!"

It's funny, but this is a real problem in the modern church.

I want you to see what this "problem" is. In our human capacity we look at this and say, "You know what? This is the container you were shaped to be, and the Lord's going to equip you and help you do what you're supposed to do. So you go wait tables in the name of Jesus." Yet the Holy Spirit's intention was never for that person to *be limited to* waiting tables.

We've had a brief look at Stephen, now let's check Phillip out. We know how Stephen's life ended in Acts chapter 7— he gave his life as a martyr. In Acts we read that Phillip went down to the city of Samaria. Remember, he was a guy who was supposed to be waiting tables:

> ⁵ Philip went down to the city of Samaria and proclaimed to them the Christ. ⁶ And the crowds with one accord paid attention to what was being said by Philip, when they heard him and saw the signs that he did. ⁷ For unclean spirits, crying out with a loud voice, came out of many who had them, and many who were paralyzed or lame were healed. ⁸ So there was much joy in that city. Acts 8:5-8

Phillip started doing crusades in Samaria and the entire city was turned the right side up for Jesus Christ, and great joy began flooding through the region. I wonder if the apostles in Jerusalem were thinking, *What in the world is this guy doing? He's supposed to be waiting tables.* I somehow doubt it—I think this is more of a modern church problem.

It was never the intention of the Holy Spirit to limit either Stephen or Phillip to one specific church duty. It was always the intention of the Holy Spirit for those two men to begin serving the church in humility, and step into and walk in their ultimate calling—the destiny God called them to while still in the wombs of their respective mothers.

Destined before Birth

There is a fascinating verse of scripture, where the Lord says to Jeremiah, "Before I formed you in the womb I knew you, and before you were born I consecrated you (or set you apart); I appointed you a prophet to the nations" (Jeremiah 1:5—addition in parentheses mine).

When Jeremiah was still a fetus, forming in his mother's womb, the Lord designated him to be a prophet. As an aside, I hope this scripture gives you a glimpse of the travesty regarding abortion in our world today. Abortion is a direct attack on the destiny the Lord speaks over a baby inside the womb. Not only is it an attempt at obstructing God's will on Earth, but it also robs those aborted babies of ever accomplishing the destiny set out for them by God.

When people say, "I'm called to do this," or "I'm called to go there," they're actually just realizing the call that was placed upon their life inside their mother's womb.

Getting back to Stephen and Phillip, God never had any intention of limiting these men to just waiting tables. He had every intention of expanding their ministries. What I find particularly interesting is even though Phillip turned Samaria upside down for Jesus Christ, this was not the completion of his future destiny. Some years later, toward the end of Phillip's life, Paul was traveling through Caesarea with Luke and they visited Phillip at his home. This is how Luke describes it: "[8] On the next day we departed and came to Caesarea, and we entered the house of Philip the evangelist, who was one of the seven, and stayed with him. [9] He had four unmarried daughters, who prophesied" (Acts 21:8-9). This was the destiny spoken over him in his mother's womb—Phillip the evangelist, one of the seven *whose daughters all prophesied!* Isn't that a remarkable testimony?

Now consider *you* have a destiny that was spoken over you in your mother's womb by Almighty God, and *this destiny is unleashed through the baptism of the Holy Spirit.*

The apostles had an idea for the immediate need they perceived—they decided to raise some people up to serve those in need, so they could continue doing the very important task of studying the Word and teaching. This is how churches roll; it's what we do. We identify problems and find solutions. I often tell folks, "Damage control is eighty percent of a pastor's work," which is actually a good thing because we're typically innovating, trying to find new ways to meet people's needs, whatever they might be. Whether needs of the soul, physical needs, or spiritual needs, we find people and we recognize the Spirit of the Lord in them and upon them, and we try to put these people into the right places. Sometimes, though, as pastors we are tempted to control the process and say, "Okay, now that you have your paradigm—your construct—operate only within that and do a good job."

If we're not careful to be yielded to the Holy Spirit, we may actually never release people into their full destiny. It's crucial to remember, every single person has a destiny that was spoken over them in their mother's womb by the Lord Himself, and that destiny 100% involves the baptism into and infilling of the Holy Spirit.

In your current life right now you might think that's not possible. You may think, *I'm just trying to survive, let alone walk into a destiny.* What you have to you realize, though, is the enemy of this world—the enemy of your soul—wants to keep you in a place where you do not recognize the destiny God has given to you. He formed you to be a bright light shining powerfully into your community. You *do* have a destiny, and in the next chapter you will discover how the Holy Spirit is the One Who will help you step into it, and fulfill it.

Receive the
Holy Spirit
Chapter Four

———❦———

L et's have a look now at how you can take a step in the right direction to find the destiny God has spoken over your life. In this chapter, I want to point out the difference between being *sealed* by the Holy Spirit and *desiring* the Holy Spirit. This piece of information is really important. In fact, it's critical. As we read the passage below, bear in mind that Phillip had been in Samaria turning the city upside down for Jesus:

> [14] Now when the apostles at Jerusalem heard that Samaria had received the word of God, they sent to them Peter and John, [15] who came down and prayed for them that they might receive the Holy Spirit, [16] for he had not yet fallen on any of them, but they had only been baptized in the name of the Lord Jesus. [17] Then they laid their hands on them and they received the Holy Spirit. Acts 8:14-17

The word "received" occurs three times in these three verses, and yet there are two different meanings applied to this word in Greek, that are not conveyed in English. It's extremely important for us to understand and distinguish between these two different meanings. Recognizing these two different Greek words used here will open your eyes, enabling you to see what is necessary to be baptized in the Holy Spirit.

In the first instance, in verse 14, the word "received" is written in the original Greek as *dechomai*. This is a passive verb that indicates a welcome reception of whatever is being offered. The literal meaning is "to receive with *ready reception* what is offered[11]."

In verses 15 and 17, on the other hand, a different meaning applies, where the word "received" is translated *lambano,* which is an active aggressive verb, suggesting a self-prompted taking. The literal definition of *lambano* means: "to take, lay hold of; to receive[12]."

So when in verse 14 the apostles heard that Samaria had received (*dechomai*) the Word of God, it means they had received it by deliberate and ready reception—they had *accepted* the message of salvation. It's as if while hearing the gospel, it had an impact on them, and they felt something happen within themselves when they received it. This is what happens with the Word of God, it's what happens at the point of salvation. It is the human heart being the ready and good soil Jesus spoke of in the parable of the sower in Matthew 13. When you receive Jesus Christ as your Savior, it's a work done outside of you; all you're doing is receiving the work. It's a near-passive or static acceptance of the truth that leads to salvation. As we continue reading, though, the difference in meaning between *dechomai* and *lambano* becomes very apparent.

In verse 15 when Peter and John prayed for those in Samaria that they might "receive" the Holy Spirit, the Greek word used is *lambano,* meaning "to reach out," or "to grab hold of and pull in." It's different because in the first instance *(dechomai)* they received the gospel message because the Word of the Lord had an impact on them. You could almost say salvation was thrust upon them, and they received it (they could have rejected it). In the second and third instances (verses 15 and 17), the word *lambano* is used because the infilling of the Holy Spirit is an active process—we need to reach out and take hold of Him; we need to desire Him and draw Him in.

When you become a believer in Jesus Christ, the Holy Spirit resurrects your spirit and makes His home in you. In fact, Ephesians tells us:

[13] In him you also, when you heard the word of truth, the gospel of your salvation, and believed in him, were sealed with the promised Holy Spirit, [14] who is the guarantee of our inheritance until we acquire possession of it, to the praise of his glory. Ephesians 1:13-14

Not one of us sealed ourselves. It was an involuntary part of the salvation process. When you accepted Jesus Christ as your Savior you had no say in the matter; it was the work of the Holy Spirit within salvation. If you're a believer in Christ, the *Holy Spirit* sealed you, guaranteeing your inheritance, which is your gift from God.

Now, distinct from the Holy Spirit's indwelling, what I'm saying is there is a baptism into the *power and fire* of the Holy Spirit. The Holy Spirit lives within the believer—we are joined to God through Him—but that doesn't mean we are *filled* with His presence. This is evident by the frequent works of our flesh.

When we invite the Holy Spirit to fill us—to completely overtake and fill our spirit being—when we're baptized in

—⊰※⊱—

Distinct from the Holy Spirit's indwelling, there is a baptism into the power and fire of the Holy Spirit.

the Holy Spirit with supernatural evidence, it is not involuntary… it is an *entirely voluntary process*. It's you who actively asks for His infilling, and it is you who then reaches out to receive or take hold of *(lambano)* this gift. You *actively* participate in fulfilling your desire for the Holy Spirit to move upon you and fill you.

I wanted to test this distinction between the two Greek words, so I searched for other scriptural examples. This is another passage from the book of Acts:

> [1] And it happened that while Apollos was at Corinth, Paul passed through the inland country and came to Ephesus. There he found some disciples. [2] And he said to them, "Did you receive the Holy Spirit when you believed?" And they said, "No, we have not even heard that there is a Holy Spirit." [3] And he said, "Into what then were you baptized?" They said, "Into John's baptism." [4] And Paul said, "John baptized with the baptism of repentance, telling the people to believe in the one who was to come after him, that is, Jesus." [5] On hearing this, they were baptized in the name of the Lord Jesus. [6] And when Paul had laid his hands on them, the Holy Spirit came on them, and they began speaking in tongues and prophesying. Acts 19:1-6

When Paul asked, "Did you receive the Holy Spirit?" the word used for "receive" is once again *lambano*. Paul was asking them, "Did you desire and hunger for the Holy Spirit

36

to fill you? Have you actively reached out and grasped hold of Him?" This example confirms that *lambano* means to ask for, to desire the Holy Spirit.

Let's look at three other verses that shed more light on this subject:

"If you then, who are evil, know how to give good gifts to your children, how much more will the heavenly Father give the Holy Spirit to those who *ask* him!" (Luke 11:13—emphasis mine). This scripture makes it clear we receive the Holy Spirit by asking the Father to fill us with His Spirit. This leads us to consider a few questions: "Is there room in your intellect to receive the Holy Spirit? Is there room within the emotional aspect of your being for the infilling of the Holy Spirit? Is there room in your spirit and in your body for the Holy Spirit?"

This is what James has to say about desiring wisdom, but I believe it applies to anything we desire from the Lord, and the manner in which we ask God for these things:

⁶ But let him ask in faith, with no doubting, for the one who doubts is like a wave of the sea that is driven and tossed by the wind. ⁷ For that person must not suppose that he will receive anything from the Lord. James 1:6-7

This scripture makes it clear we are to have an active, expectant desire God will give us what we ask if it aligns with His Word. We cannot ask God in a doubtful manner.

Yet another reference to receiving the Holy Spirit was made by Jesus in John's gospel:

³⁷ On the last day of the feast, the great day, Jesus stood up and cried out, "If anyone thirsts, let him come to me and drink. ³⁸ Whoever believes in me, as the Scripture has

37

said, 'Out of his heart will flow rivers of living water.'"
[39] Now this he said about the Spirit, whom those who believed in him were to receive, for as yet the Spirit had not been given, because Jesus was not yet glorified. John 7:37-39

Can you imagine being a guest at a holiday banquet and somebody stands up and yells this? It may seem awkward but Jesus evidently wanted the other guests to take note of what He had to say. As we see in the Greek translation, Jesus once more used the context of the word *lambano* when He spoke of the Spirit, which those who believed in Him would later "receive."

I hope these scriptures and the meaning of the original Greek words shed some light on this important subject, and in relation to this, I would like you to consider an important question as you continue reading. Have you been baptized in the Holy Spirit? I'm not asking you if you are a believer in Jesus Christ. I assume you are, because I believe the only way to be baptized in the Holy Spirit is if you already *are* a believer in Jesus Christ.

An Ongoing Hunger
We'll look at this in more detail in later chapters but I want to suggest that once you have been baptized in the Holy Spirit there's an ongoing asking, a continual hunger and desire to be filled with the Holy Spirit. A continual infilling, if you will. At least, this happens in my life and I see it reflected in scripture too. At Pentecost the infilling of the Holy Spirit happened in such a powerful way (Acts chapter 2), but in Acts chapter 4 in another upper room event we are told, "they were all filled with the Holy Spirit" (Acts 4:31b). This shows how the infilling of the Spirit happened again. It's an ongoing infilling preceded by an ongoing hunger; an

ongoing desire.

When I was first filled with the Spirit (when I was baptized in the Holy Spirit), I had been seriously hungering for the Lord. I wanted a deeper relationship with Him but I recognized there was persistent sin in my life. I hated the sin but I didn't seem to have the power to rid my life of it; it felt like I just couldn't do it on my own. I

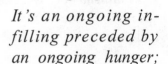

It's an ongoing in-filling preceded by an ongoing hunger; an ongoing desire.

remember hearing from God—it was one of the first times I heard the Lord—not audibly but in my spirit, I heard the Lord speak, saying, "David, here's what I want you to do…"

It was a time of testing and refining; the Lord had asked me to start getting up at 3:30 in the morning to pursue Him. I accepted this request, knowing I would be on a sleeping fast—I would be fasting sleep-time instead of food. So I started my fast, waking up early in the morning. I would start the day with coffee, but there is no coffee strong enough to keep me awake at 3:30 in the morning. Still, I persisted because I was desperate, but my fast stretched on for a whole month.

At the end of that month, I remember on one particular day I had my elbows on my knees and my head in my hands, totally exasperated. I was tired and frustrated, but the Lord understands all our emotions. I remember calling out to the Lord, saying, "Lord, if you don't do something… please Lord, You know I want You, I long for You, I want more of You… but if You don't meet with me I'm just going back to bed."

I recall sitting in my seat suddenly thinking I was starting to get sick. There were chills running up and down my body. I felt goosebumps rising on my skin… and then it happened—I knew I was in the presence of the Lord. I *knew* it. I unmistakably felt His presence. I felt Him as He began speaking to me in my spirit, and I fellowshipped serenely and powerfully with the Lord.

The best way I can describe it is to present an image of what I experienced: as I sat there, it felt as though I was a baby in a highchair. The Holy Spirit was there holding a baby spoon filled with apple sauce, or some nutritious spiritual fruit, and He began to spoon-feed me.

If you've ever had the privilege of feeding a little baby you'll know how messy it can be—food is usually smeared all over the baby's face in the process, all over the bib, and all over the tray. This is what it felt like to me. I began saying things I didn't understand (at least not in English), and then the Spirit of the Lord would respond. I didn't know what it was at the time, it was simply an impulse I perceived. Of course, I know now it was the Holy Spirit. I would say something, and then the Spirit of the Lord would say, "David, here's what you just said." I would say something else, and again the Holy Spirit would say, "David, here's what you just said." Remember, I *knew* this was the Lord.

I was engaged in intimate fellowship with the Holy Spirit. I didn't know it then, not having experienced it so powerfully before, but I knew I was right in the presence of God. I will share more with you on this subject as we progress through the book, but I want you to know, the baptism of the Holy Spirit is available to anyone who desires and asks for this gift from God.

Here's what this experience taught me: I was filled with a supernatural power at that point in time, enabling me to look at the various sins in my life and say, "No! In the name of Jesus I have overcome this sin." From this point forward there was sufficient power in my life to overcome these sins. Am I perfect? No. Do I have power to overcome sin and am I more aware of that power? Yes and yes again!

That's why Jesus said, in Acts 1:8: "You will have power." I desperately needed God's power, and you do too— everyone needs it. The transforming work of Jesus Christ occurs in us and through us as we touch the lives of people around us with His power.

Since that day, I've never been the same. I've become uniquely aware of the presence of the Holy Spirit and the power of the Holy Spirit. If God allowed me to be filled with His Spirit, He will certainly fill you too. It is for this reason I offer it to you. I want nothing short of you walking in the fullness of God's Spirit. God also wants you to have His Holy Spirit so you can walk into the destiny He has for you.

I totally understand you might have reservations about this process but I'm asking you to step forward in faith today. I also want you to understand in advance, when you submit to the Holy Spirit, He may touch your body in ways you don't expect. I remember having chills going up and down my body early that morning, and at the time I was thinking, *I don't want chills right now, I don't want to get sick, what is this? This is weird.* Yet I didn't get sick; it was the Holy Spirit, and that was what He chose to do. Other physical experiences may take place, but that's also okay because it's the Holy Spirit touching you in a personal way.

When you come into contact with the supernatural presence of God, it is understandable that your body will have some kind of reaction. You might start crying. On certain occasions I have laid my hands on somebody and prayed they would be filled with the Holy Spirit and in response they started crying. I'm good with that as it's a completely natural response.

Sometimes when people are filled with the Spirit they start laughing, and I'm good with that too, because it's another natural response. Joy is a fruit of the Spirit. Individuals usually respond differently to the Holy Spirit. He is God and He has control, but we ought to be hungering after Him and submitting to the Holy Spirit all the time. Most importantly, please don't be afraid to receive the power of the Holy Spirit in your life.

As you continue reading, I pray you will keep learning, growing, and walking forward to meet with the Holy Spirit. Once you have accepted Jesus as Lord of your life, this is where the Spirit of the Lord wants to start His journey with you.

Refilled with the Holy Spirit
Chapter Five

Would you agree the Holy Spirit has the power to heal? I believe He does, and I also believe this power exists within all of us who claim the Lord Jesus as Savior. Speaking about this same power, Paul said, "If the Spirit of him who raised Jesus from the dead dwells in you, he who raised Christ Jesus from the dead will also give life to your mortal bodies through his Spirit who dwells in you" (Romans 8:11).

We all obviously have life in our *bodies* prior to being saved, as dead people cannot be saved. So, Paul is clearly not speaking about simply being technically alive in our physical body—having a pulse; he's talking about bringing to you wholeness of life when you're ill and when your body is broken. The same power that raised Jesus' broken, dead body raised Him from the dead in perfect health and full of life. Just as the Holy Spirit raised Jesus, He'll raise you up too.

There are many related benefits to being filled with the Holy Spirit, and in this chapter we will continue unpacking passages of scripture relating to the Holy Spirit's infilling and the benefits thereof, and we will continue studying the baptism of the Holy Spirit.

There are three things about the baptism of the Holy Spirit I want to place before you and then I want to look at the word "baptism." What does it mean? Why did Jesus choose that word over many other words He could have chosen? We will be basing this study on Acts 1:5b, where Jesus said, "You will be baptized with the Holy Spirit not many days from now."

Why did He choose the word "baptized"? It's an interesting word, especially when you begin to understand the significance of the word. Let's start by looking at the phrase "being filled with the Holy Spirit." I will point to three concepts I want you to entertain as we dig in.

We will start with Acts 4 and here's point number 1:

Evangelism and Boldness
Evangelism and boldness were coupled with the filling of the Holy Spirit. Before we read the passage from Acts, let me give you some brief background history. Peter and John were heading to church and on the way they stopped to heal a man. The notoriety of his miraculous healing began to spread, so the religious leaders of the time arrested Peter and John and put them in jail. They could not find any reason to keep them detained, though, so they had

> *Evangelism and boldness were coupled with the filling of the Holy Spirit.*

to release the two apostles.

After having spent a period of time in jail, the apostles went back to where the church gathered and they found them praying, so Peter and John joined in. This is what they prayed: "²⁹ And now, Lord, look upon their threats and grant to your servants to continue to speak your word with all *boldness*, ³⁰ while you stretch out your hand to heal, and signs and wonders are performed through the name of your holy servant Jesus" (Acts 4:29-30—my emphasis).

They were asking the Holy Spirit to be active in the name of the Lord Jesus, but they were also praying for more boldness. I find this quite interesting because in Acts 1:8 Jesus said they would "receive power when the Holy Spirit" had come upon them. From these two scriptures it appears to me that this power comes about when the apostles *used* the boldness and authority given to them by the Holy Spirit.

Refilled with the Holy Spirit
The second thing I want to point out is the disciples, the apostles, and all those at the prayer meeting were *refilled* with the Holy Spirit. This means the infilling of the Spirit was not a one-time event. Remember, at Pentecost the Holy Spirit was poured out on the believers in the upper room, and suddenly tongues that looked like flames rested upon their heads and they began to speak in other tongues (paraphrase of Acts 2:1-4). Other people who heard them speaking in different languages said, "They're drunk."

The apostle Peter immediately defended the believers, saying, "They're not drunk, they're filled with the Holy Spirit" (paraphrase of Acts 2:15). What's interesting is most scholars believe Acts 4 took place within the same year as Acts 2. It all happened in a very short period of time. Note that in Acts 4 they were praying and they were filled with the Holy Spirit: "And when they had prayed, the place in which they were gathered together was shaken, and they were all filled with the Holy Spirit and continued to speak the word of God with boldness" (Acts 4:31).

Notice the believers weren't shaking, but rather the *house* was shaking "and they were all filled with the Holy Spirit." Now wait a second—how could they be filled with the Holy Spirit if they had already been filled less than a year before at Pentecost? What's the Holy Spirit trying to tell us? He's telling us it's a good thing to be *continuously* filled with the Holy Spirit.

I don't know about you, but I pray on a regular basis, "Lord, fill me to overflowing with the Holy Spirit." I pray this often. It's one of my regular prayers because I know myself. I know what I'm capable of, and how my flesh can take over. I know this human weakness about myself, so I pray to be filled with the Holy Spirit often.

What does it mean to be filled with the Holy Spirit? It means love, joy, peace, patience, kindness, goodness, faithfulness, gentleness, and self-control all well up within me. This fruit of the Spirit (Galatians 5:22-23), which are spiritual manifestations, are not natural within our human nature. What *is* natural is for me to be an angry ogre. What's natural is for me to take first, so I can have what's mine. It's natural for me to bypass the needs of other people and take care of myself. Yet, when I accepted Jesus as my Savior, the Father planted the Holy Spirit within me and He activated the fruit of the Holy Spirit. Now when I seek the Holy Spirit to well up within me and manifest this fruit, this has nothing to do with our world. The Holy Spirit is not from this world.

46

As a matter of fact, the fruit of the Holy Spirit is the culture of Heaven! This fruit is present in Heaven all the time and it will never be adulterated. The culture of Heaven comes down to Earth through the Holy Spirit and lives inside of me. That's what the Kingdom of Heaven is. It's learning how to live in Heaven's culture—in the Spirit—here and now.

It is so special that God would take the culture of Heaven, put it inside you and say, "Live! Do so with power and authority!" When we are filled continuously we begin to walk in power and authority, and we see life-changes happen. It's not just us who see the change, but other people see it too—they look at us and say, "You're drunk!" just like they said at Pentecost. But we're not drunk, we're filled with the Holy Spirit. We have love, joy, peace, patience, kindness, goodness, faithfulness, gentleness, and self-control.

This is why I continually pray, "Lord, fill me to overflowing." I pray this because my flesh is continually nipping at my heels, just as your flesh does to you. There's a lot of nasty, mean stuff that goes on in this world. In the natural it makes sense for you to be angry, unforgiving, bitter, and resentful. It makes sense to steal what you need, and to simply look at people and not trust them. Walking in fear makes natural sense because of all of the horrible things that could happen, yet this fear is what we war against and why we need to be filled with the Holy Spirit *on a regular basis.*

I believe it is for this very reason the Holy Spirit put that verse about the second infilling in the book of Acts. We know the believers were filled with the Holy Spirit less than a year prior to the infilling recorded in Acts 4, yet in this chapter they're filled with the Holy Spirit once more.

My challenge to you is to be filled with the Holy Spirit. Be filled to overflowing with the power that raised Jesus Christ from the dead. It's yours! It's yours to actively reach out and take hold of.

Baptized in Jesus and Baptized in the Holy Spirit

The third point I want to make is the most important: after you are baptized in the name of Jesus you *must* be baptized in the Holy Spirit. This is important for you to grasp before we go any further in trying to understand what baptism means, and what the implications of baptism truly are.

We have already spent some time looking at different aspects of Acts 8, where Phillip goes into Samaria and starts preaching and teaching. People were being saved, miracles were being done, and people were being water baptized. Then something really interesting happened—the apostles in Jerusalem heard what was going on, so they sent Peter and John to Samaria. There's a reason for these leaders going to Samaria and I think we ought to take notice of it:

> [12] But when they believed Philip as he preached good news about the kingdom of God and the name of Jesus Christ, they were baptized, both men and women. [13] Even Simon himself believed, and after being baptized he continued with Philip. And seeing signs and great miracles performed, he was amazed.
>
> [14] Now when the apostles at Jerusalem heard that Samaria had received the word of God, they sent to them Peter and John, [15] who came down and prayed for them that they might receive the Holy Spirit, [16] for he had not yet fallen on any of them, but they had only been baptized in the name of the Lord Jesus. [17] Then they laid their hands on them and they received the Holy Spirit. Acts 8:12-17

This is what I call an awesome day of ministry! Think

about it—after preaching to the people, *the entire city* gets saved and miracles are happening everywhere. At this point most people would think, *Okay, I'm going home now. I'm going to have lunch, and I'm taking a killer nap! Today has been an awesome day.*

Yet the Holy Spirit didn't stop there… He wouldn't stop there. Phillip was probably thinking, *This has been a great day!* Yet Peter and John went to the city even after the Samaritan people had been saved and baptized in the name of Jesus, with great signs and miracles being performed. The Samaritans probably saw limbs grow back and eyes opened—the day was nothing short of amazing!

Most modern believers would probably walk away from this time of ministry saying, "That was one of the coolest days in the house of God I've ever seen." Yet the Holy Spirit made sure those in authority went back and laid hands on the new believers. Why? Because they needed to be baptized and filled with the Holy Spirit. I find this very significant. Most of us would consider this a job well done—I mean miracles had

The Holy Spirit wanted these new believers to be filled with His Spirit so they could start transforming others.

taken place—but the Holy Spirit knew it was critical these new believers walk in His full power, so He sent Peter and John to finish the job. He wanted these new believers to be *filled* with His Spirit so they could start transforming others.

According to Acts 8, it's *imperative* that you be filled to overflowing with the Holy Spirit.

This concept may be a challenge for some of you. It may

not fit with your theology. It may tax your intellect or baffle your logic, and that's okay. I was there too but the more I study scripture the more I find it's essential for believers to be filled with the Holy Spirit.

Let me give you one more example from Luke 3, which takes place very early in the ministry of our Lord Jesus:

> [21] Now when all the people were baptized, and when Jesus also had been baptized and was praying, the heavens were opened, [22] and the Holy Spirit descended on him in bodily form, like a dove; and a voice came from heaven, "You are my beloved Son; with you I am well pleased." Luke 3:21-22

The chapter continues by presenting the genealogy of Jesus, but the next chapter starts with these words: "And Jesus, *full of the Holy Spirit,* returned from the Jordan and was led by the Spirit in the wilderness" (Luke 4:1—my emphasis).

I want you to see the progression of how the ministry of Jesus unfolded. Jesus came to John the Baptist who baptized Him in water, and then almost immediately—as He came up out of the water and started praying—the Holy Spirit descended upon Him and Jesus was filled with the Holy Spirit. The very next action presented by Luke details how the Holy Spirit led Him into the wilderness.

My thoughts on the matter initially went like this, *Of all the people on Earth, if any person did not need to be baptized or didn't need to be filled with the Holy Spirit, it would be Jesus.* Yet Jesus willingly submitted Himself to both processes. Looking at this from a human standpoint, I first thought He didn't need to submit to either process, but then I realized from a scriptural standpoint it was necessary for Jesus to partake in both processes. Jesus had to be water-baptized and then filled with the Holy Spirit not only to fulfill the Father's will for His life but also to set an example for you and for me.

This is just my opinion, but I believe it is unlikely for a person to be baptized in the Holy Spirit without first being water-baptized. Because of the command given by Peter in Acts 2, and the requirement assigned to water baptism, a person knowingly rejecting water baptism is willfully disobedient. It doesn't really make sense that this person would reject water baptism and accept the baptism of the Holy Spirit.

Being water-baptized is an act of obedience and if I'm in defiance of this process, the Holy Spirit will not fill me with overflowing love, joy, peace, patience, and all the good things He wants spread abroad. He simply won't do it. When we think about water baptism, it doesn't seem to make much sense in our natural, physical world. When we consider it from a natural viewpoint we can easily start thinking, *It doesn't make any sense, so I'm not going to do it. It seems kind of strange to get dunked under water by another believer… then people start clapping and jumping up and down. I'm just not into doing things in public, so I'm not going to do it. Besides that, I was baptized as a baby, I'm fine.*

Jesus was water baptized and then He was filled with the Holy Spirit.

This kind of thinking leads to us cutting ourselves off from further blessing. Jesus was water baptized and then He was filled with the Holy Spirit. The water baptism is extremely significant and has very specific symbolism attached. In this chapter I first wanted to build a foundation regarding the importance of the infilling and refilling of the Holy Spirit, and I also wanted to emphasize the benefits we receive from this infilling. In the next chapter I will explain the significance and symbolism of the various baptisms taught in scripture and their implication for the baptism of the Holy Spirit.

Three Baptisms
Chapter Six

Let's take a few minutes to explore the meaning of this word "baptism." The Greek word used is *baptizo,* which is not that different to English. The literal translation of the word *baptizo* is a transitive verb meaning "I wash." Because the Greek word was transliterated into English, meaning it was left in its original form due to possible controversy regarding meaning, we find various interpretations attached to *baptizo*. Some English words used to describe *baptizo* are "immersed" and "dipped," so it follows that water baptism represents dying to yourself (the old you) and being raised in Christ (the new you). Subsequently, being immersed in water can be likened to death by drowning. If there is any doubt about baptism being a full representation of death, listen to Paul's description of baptism given in two separate passages:

> ² By no means! How can we who died to sin still live in it? ³ Do you not know that all of us who have been baptized into Christ Jesus were baptized into his death? ⁴ We were buried therefore with him by baptism into death, in order that, just as Christ was raised from the

dead by the glory of the Father, we too might walk in newness of life. Romans 6:2-4

And again, Paul's letter to the Colossians expresses the same thought with different words:

[11] In him also you were circumcised with a circumcision made without hands, by putting off the body of the flesh, by the circumcision of Christ, [12] having been buried with him in baptism, in which you were also raised with him through faith in the powerful working of God, who raised him from the dead. [13] And you, who were dead in your trespasses and the uncircumcision of your flesh, God made alive together with him, having forgiven us all our trespasses, [14] by canceling the record of debt that stood against us with its legal demands. This he set aside, nailing it to the cross. [15] He disarmed the rulers and authorities and put them to open shame, by triumphing over them in him. Colossians 2:11-15

Can you see it? It is hard to miss the implications of baptism.

So, what it means to be baptized is *you die*—the old person remains in the watery grave, and the new you is raised in Christ to new life and power. I also find it interesting that Jesus is the One Who chose those words. He chose the word "baptized" in Acts 1:5b, "For John baptized with water, but you will be baptized with the Holy Spirit not many days from now." To me this essentially means "John drowned you in

> *What it means to be baptized is you die.*

water"—you died in the water. In a similar way, you will be drowned in the Holy Spirit, meaning you will die to your flesh and your spirit will be made alive.

If baptism means "to be drowned,"[13] my thought process

follows this line: there are three baptisms in scripture and I'll share all three with you. Each of them has a death associated with it. In each of them you are drowned, and I think the first two will make a lot of sense to you, thereby validating the third one, which is the baptism of the Holy Spirit.

The Baptism of Blood
The first baptism we encounter in scripture is the baptism of blood. At the moment you're saved—when your spirit is sealed for the day of redemption—you and I are baptized in the blood of Jesus. A specific verse of scripture makes this clear: "But if we walk in the light, as he is in the light, we have fellowship with one another, and *the blood of Jesus his Son cleanses us from all sin*: (1 John 1:7—my emphasis).

This is a picture of baptism into the blood of Christ. When you accept Christ as your Savior, the penalty of your sin is washed away. It's dead and gone! Never again do you have to worry about the penalty of sin and the power of sin in your life. This means the old man—that fleshly part—he's drowned! The new man is born, and raised up with Christ! So what this means is I have power over my sins. Prior to the Lord Jesus being in my life I wanted to be a better person but I didn't have any *power* to make that happen.

When I was baptized in the blood of Jesus Christ, though, He washed my sin away. He set me up and made me righteous and whole so I could go to Heaven. I'm no longer going to hell because of my sin. My sin is washed away, and my old man—the flesh that's always hungry, always wanting to be fed—it drowned in the blood of Jesus. This is why Paul wrote: "I have been crucified with Christ. It is no longer I who live, but Christ who lives in me" (Galatians 2:20a).

The flesh is drowned, it's crucified. This is exactly

55

what I needed. Not only is the penalty of sin destroyed, but the *power* of sin is destroyed. This is such a wonderful gift because prior to my salvation in Christ, I desperately wanted to be a better man but I didn't have any real power to execute this drastic change. Without the blood of Jesus there is no hope. Now, having access to the name of Jesus, being baptized in the blood of Jesus and having the Lord Jesus' Spirit live within me, I can look at my sin and say, "No more!" I break that chain, I'm not walking down that path, and I don't believe that lie about myself anymore. I can live a free life through the blood of Jesus.

Romans 6 says this: "⁶ We know that our old self was crucified with him in order that the body of sin might be brought to nothing, so that we would no longer be enslaved to sin. ⁷ For one who has died has been set free from sin" (Romans 6:6-7). Right there we can see the blood baptism gives you the power to have sin removed. This does not mean you won't sin anymore, it means you will not be *in bondage* to it.

Now understand that you have the power to be free of sin, but if sin becomes entrenched again through patterns of behavior that recur in your life, the only reason this happens is because you say, "I want it." You're no longer a slave to this type of sinful behavior and you haven't lost your salvation, but the quality of your life will be lost—you will essentially be shipwrecking your newfound potential in Christ by not controlling your desire. Remember, the fruit of the Spirit gives you self-control.

If you willfully persist in sin after salvation, you may end up feeling as though you're not saved but the Spirit of the Lord has sealed you on the day of your redemption. Sin is painful and horrible, yet you must understand the name of Jesus Christ gives you the power to break the hold sin has in your life. I thank God for His fresh mercy every day (Lamentations 3:22-23), because scripture tells us, "So if the Son sets you free, you will be free indeed" (John 8:36).

The Baptism of Water
The second baptism is the baptism of water, which is what we're accustomed to within the body of Christ. Being baptized in water is to publicly acknowledge you are part of the Christian faith. Water baptism is an act of obedience that follows salvation.

Peter said to the first converts, "Repent and *be baptized* every one of you in the name of Jesus Christ for the forgiveness of your sins, and you will receive the gift of the Holy Spirit" (Acts 2:38—my emphasis). Why did Peter tell them to repent *and* be baptized? Repentance is really the blood baptism—you recognize your flesh has been ruling your life and you're in sin, so you repent of this and turn away from your sin. This means death to the old man, and you turn toward a life in Christ. That's the essence of repentance. Notice Peter inserted the word "and" between "repent" and "be baptized," making it clear the two actions must happen in conjunction with each other.

This leads to an important question: what does it mean to be drowned in water baptism? What dies in this particular baptism? If baptism means to be drowned or to die, what aspect of your humanity actually dies when you are publicly immersed in water baptism? Perhaps you've already figured it out... it's your *will* that dies. The only thing that would ever stop you from being water baptized is your will. It's you saying, "I won't! I choose not to. No, that's not for me. Nah, that's passé, that's old."

Your will essentially stops you from being baptized. A crucial part of water baptism is that your will must be crucified. Your will has to drown, so that when you say, "Lord, you have washed me in the blood of Jesus and now You expect me to be publicly water baptized," your spirit surrenders to this call by saying, "I will, I submit."

It doesn't make any natural sense. Many people in this world who lack faith may look at you and say, "What are you doing? Why are you being dunked in the water? That doesn't make any sense."

It doesn't have to make sense. It's what God expects of you, it's what He commanded, so your best response is to acknowledge His commandment by saying, "I will—I *will* do what *He* says, I will." *Your* will has to die. When you're water baptized, you basically surrender or subjugate your will to the Word of God. Your will is drowned. This book is about the Holy Spirit, so pay attention to Him right now. He might be nudging you to be water baptized because you haven't fulfilled this commandment as of yet. It will open the door to more blessing for you.

Baptized with the Holy Spirit

This third baptism is spoken of in scripture by Jesus:

> [4] And while staying with them he ordered them not to depart from Jerusalem, but to wait for the promise of the Father, which, he said, "you heard from me; [5] for John baptized with water, but *you will be baptized with the Holy Spirit* not many days from now." Acts 1:4-5—my emphasis

Jesus chose those words Himself, including the word "baptized." In effect He was saying, "You will be drowned in the Holy Spirit, not many days from now." While our human

58

response to this may be, "*No!* I know I don't want to be drowned, even if it is in the Holy Spirit… I'd rather take a little touch of the Holy Spirit." Yet it was Jesus who used the word "baptized," meaning "You will be drowned in the Holy Spirit." There can be no flesh-life left in you—nothing you can lay claim to. You must be drowned in the Holy Spirit, and filled with the Holy Spirit.

I know this material may not be quite the comfortable Sunday school message you're used to, but has anything comfortable lifted you out of your comfort zone yet? Has anything comfortable gained you any more spiritual power? My prayer and my desire for every person reading this book is for you to be filled with the Holy Spirit. I pray with all my heart you are filled to overflowing with Him.

Let's continue. In Acts 1:8 we read: "But you will receive power when the Holy Spirit has come upon you, and you will be my witnesses in Jerusalem and in all Judea and Samaria, and to the end of the earth."

What will people see when you interact with them? What will they sense? What will cause them to stop and look at you? They will see love, joy, peace, patience, kindness, goodness, faithfulness, gentleness, and self-control. They will see the very culture of Heaven right before their eyes. How miraculous is that?

Jesus said, "The one who conquers, I will grant him to sit with me on my throne" (Revelation 3:21a). What will we conquer? What will we overcome? The flesh. How will we do this? By surrendering to the Holy Spirit and allowing the fruit of the Holy Spirit to be a part of our being, the culture of Heaven to rise up in us. This happens when you are filled with the Holy Spirit. Be filled to overflowing with the Holy

Spirit. If you ask Him, He will surely fill you.

So, if the sins of the flesh are washed away by baptism in the blood of Jesus, and our self-will dies when we are baptized in water, what dies when we are baptized with the Holy Spirit? I think this will make sense to you. What dies and is drowned at the baptism of the Holy Spirit is fear. *Fear* dies.

To be baptized in the Holy Spirit, I have to lay my carnal intellect down. The logic I lean on? I have to lay that down too. My dogma? I have to lay that down too. I have to lay *everything* down at the feet of Jesus. I must want and desire the Holy Spirit more than I want my own intellect and logic—more than anything I have. Isn't that how we came to Christ in the first place? Didn't we come to Jesus needing a Savior? So we reach out and we say, "I need a Savior. Jesus save me." I didn't understand all the intricacies of salvation, I just knew I needed a Savior so I asked Him and He forgave me. Should I be any different in pursuing the Holy Spirit? Everything I have been, currently am, and hope to be, I lay before God and ask Him to reveal more of who He is through the Holy Spirit.

Now, decades later I know so much more than I did back then, but I still haven't even scraped the surface of what salvation is nor what the love of God truly means. I'll figure it out in the gazillion years I have in eternity, but for right now I know a little bit more.

No one goes to the Father with full knowledge, otherwise it wouldn't be faith—you would just know. Faith is *not understanding,* faith is *not knowing,* but faith is recognizing that you need God, so you make a decision by faith to step out and believe. The same thing happened for you when you were saved, as it does when you decide to go into the water to be baptized. You stepped out in faith thinking *I'm not sure exactly what all of this means, I just know the Word of God says I need to do it, so I will do it.* You know you need it, and you submit to God. You do it not through self-will, but by aligning your will with the will of God.

Being filled with the Holy Spirit is an *identical* act of faith to being baptized in the blood of Jesus, and being baptized in water. The biggest thing you have to overcome is your fear. *What will He do to me? What will happen? Will I start speaking in tongues? Will there be a flame of fire over my head? Will I fall on the floor?*

I don't know and neither do you! This is a part of the hurdle you must jump, the barrier you must break through in faith. It's a part of the surrendering that allows us to say, "Thank you Lord. I simply receive. I receive love, joy, peace, patience, kindness... Holy Spirit fill me, body, soul, and spirit, so I might be what You want me to be. Walk me into my destiny."

Fear has to die; faith has to rise up. You have to take a step in faith, strongly desiring to be filled with the Holy Spirit, just like you wanted salvation. Maybe you need to fast and pray to get your flesh out of the way. Maybe take a week off work to focus on receiving this priceless Gift? What is He worth to you? What is Acts 2 power worth in your life? How will it change your life?

> *Fear has to die; faith has to rise up.*

I want to walk you through a passage of scripture that

made no sense to me for many years, until I began thinking about the baptism of the Holy Spirit. The passage speaks about Jesus and it has recently come alive for me: "This is he who came by water and blood—Jesus Christ; not by the water only but by the water and the blood. And the Spirit is the one who testifies, *because the Spirit is the truth"* (1 John 5:6—my emphasis).

In verses 7-8 John says, "⁷ For there are three that testify: ⁸ *the Spirit and the water and the blood*; and these three agree" (1 John 5:7-8—my emphasis). Aren't these the three baptisms referenced in scripture? The Spirit and the water and the blood. Notice verse 8 ends by saying, "and these three agree." The translation there goes beyond the simple meaning we associate with the word "agree." It transcends the fact that these three elements are in agreement with each other. What the author is pointing out is that these three elements of life are real! These three elements exist; take notice of them, because they're a part of God's plan.

Notice that the author didn't leave the Spirit out of this verse. You might rationalize, "We're good with the blood and the water" but the Spirit is included too, and we're often less comfortable with Him in the picture. John continues: "Whoever believes in the Son of God has the testimony in himself" (John 5:10a). What testimony is being referenced in this verse? The testimony is the fact that God gave us eternal life and this life is in His Son.

The Holy Spirit testifies in you, about you. How do you think the early believers received their power? Do you remember that New Testament power demonstrated by how they went from city to city and people were baptized, and towns were turned right side up for Jesus? Where did the power come from? The power is the Holy Spirit *in* them, testifying about the fact that He's in them. He is giving them the confidence and authority.

This theme of the Spirit testifying of His presence within us through our words and deeds is raised again in Paul's letter to the Romans:

> [15] For you did not receive the spirit of slavery to fall back into fear, but you have received the Spirit of adoption as sons, by whom we cry, "Abba! Father!" [16] The Spirit himself bears witness with our spirit that we are children of God, [17] and if children, then heirs—heirs of God and fellow heirs with Christ, provided we suffer with him in order that we may also be glorified with him. Romans 8:15-17

Fear is mentioned as something that people slip back into. This is the part of us that has to die; we walk our Christian life out in faith, not doubting. Take note of verse 16: "The Spirit himself bears witness with our spirit that we are children of God." There it is again, the Spirit is testifying—testifying in you about who you are and who you're not. Just consider who God is, and as His children we are heirs—heirs of God and fellow-heirs with Christ. What a great testimony being testified through us by God Himself!

Verse 17 closes by saying: "Provided we suffer with him in order that we may also be glorified with him." I believe the word "suffer" means we have to be drowned. Our old man has to be drowned, our will has to be drowned, and our fear has to be drowned. This all refers to suffering, and it is a lot of suffering yet it's the only way you will be filled with the Holy Spirit. A lot of drowning had to take place in the Bible, right? A lot of drowning has to take place in our life too.

My encouragement to you is be filled with the Holy Spirit. Be filled to overflowing.

Many people are suffering, and my heart goes out to you because you're fighting as much as you can to make it through this world. Still, you keep getting hit on the chin and kicked in the shins, and gut-punched, and you're suffering. One thing after another keeps coming at you, and you're going through life with your strength almost completely depleted.

Some of you are under the water at this point but you're coming up for your last gulp of air. You're a believer, but you're fighting hard for your last breath, refusing to drown. Let me ask you one important question: "What if the same power that raised Jesus Christ from the dead… what if that power raised you from the deadness of your own works? Your own intellect. Your own dogma. What if that same power was unleashed within you? What if…?"

Not only will it restore your life, but other people will take notice and say, "What is going on inside of you?"

The answer is "Jesus! The risen Christ within me is what's going on."

"How did you do that?" they'll ask.

"Well, my flesh is dead. I live for Christ and my will is *His* to command."

This is when you change lives. It is when the Holy Spirit in you overflows to other people. When the love of God fills me it almost brings me to the point of tears, as I feel His love for others. The fruit of the Spirit: love, joy, peace, patience, kindness, goodness, faithfulness, gentleness, and self-control—the things I was unable to do I can now do, because God lives in me.

Would you like some of the fruit of God's Holy Spirit in your life?

When you are filled with the Holy Spirit you will begin to understand how the disciples felt when God sent them out with power. That's why Jesus said, "Not many days from now, you will be filled with power." This power was not just for the disciples, it's for you too! It's your life, and it's there for the asking, it's there for the taking—it's yours. Even though I might be overstating this because I know how great the need is, I still have to say it one more time: be filled with the Holy Spirit.

> *This power was not just for the disciples, it's for you too!*

If you are ready to receive Him, let's pray together. Right now as you're reading these words just open up your body, soul, and spirit, and read these words aloud:

Lord, I breathe You in. Don't let anything in me stop me from being filled with Your Spirit. All of it. I want the culture of Heaven within me. I want the Holy Spirit to live within me, through me, and to empower me. Lord God, there are areas of my life I feel the need to speak the name of Jesus into, even though until now I haven't felt the strength to enable me to do it. Fill me with Your Holy Spirit that I may speak into those things and see those chains broken.

Father we thank You that Your Word is true and the only way we can approach You to receive from You is by faith. We freely admit we do not have this figured out.

Nobody possesses the knowledge to explain this in

absolute detail. Nobody is able to ensure everybody is willing to simply accept the power of the Holy Spirit, but Lord we come to You with our lack of understanding. We lack, we walk in unbelief, we struggle at surrendering to You, Holy Spirit; but Lord our faith compels us to step over the threshold and ask You to please fill us with the power we need to live. We need You so much. Thank You Jesus. We pray in Jesus name. Amen.

As it is taught in the New Testament, it may be that you need a refilling of the Holy Spirit. I know I do—almost every day. I keep going back, asking for more and more, because things happen in life and I need God's strength within me.

It should also be noted that Peter and John went to Samaria and laid hands on people to receive the baptism of the Holy Spirit. It's one thing to sit in a seat and say, "Please fill me Holy Spirit," but it can sometimes be more effective to have some church elders lay hands on you. This may be exactly what you need today.

Whether you've been a Christian your whole life or if this is something entirely new to you, if you don't feel capable of succeeding in this process then ask the church elders in your area to lay hands on you and pray over you to receive the baptism of the Holy Spirit. Ask them to pray so you will be filled to overflowing with the Holy Spirit.

Honor the Holy Spirit

Chapter Seven

In this chapter I will present a concept regarding the Holy Spirit that we do not often associate with Him, even though scripture speaks directly to this topic. I believe the neglect of this critical Christian virtue is one of the reasons we don't see healings and miracles as widespread occurrences today, even though healings and miracles occur frequently in scripture.

This first passage of scripture sets the scene:

¹ He went away from there and came to his hometown, and his disciples followed him. ² And on the Sabbath he began to teach in the synagogue, and many who heard him were astonished, saying, "Where did this man get these things? What is the wisdom given to him? How are such mighty works done by his hands?" Mark 6:1-2

What I want you to see here is the astonishment felt by the people of Nazareth was soon replaced by a second sentiment. Marvel at the miraculous works soon turned to questioning Jesus' pedigree. When these questions were left unchecked in light of the obvious evidence of the miraculous, their interrogation of Jesus soon turned the people of His hometown sour toward Him: "Is not this the carpenter, the son of Mary and brother of James and Joses and Judas and Simon? And are not his sisters here with us?" And they took offense at him" (Mark 6:3).

Understand that these people took offense at *God!* They took offense at the Miracle-worker; the Messiah. These are His relatives and neighbors from childhood! How did Jesus respond to their offense? "And Jesus said to them, 'A prophet is not without honor, except in his hometown and among his relatives and in his own household'" (Mark 6:4). I find what follows next to be one of the most astounding verses in the Bible: "And *he could do no mighty work there*, except that he laid his hands on a few sick people and healed them" (Mark 6:5—my emphasis).

How is it even possible that Jesus couldn't do miracles in the town of His upbringing? It is clear to me that Jesus wants us to understand why miracles were so scarce in His hometown so He actually identified the reason His power was limited in Nazareth. Reading this scripture today, we look at the world around us and ask, "I wonder if miracles are dead? Did they disappear with the apostles? Did they go away when the Bible was compiled, when the canon of holy scripture was sealed? Is that what happened?"

Nowhere in scripture— not one place—does God say He modified His plan.

I want to encourage you, nowhere in scripture—not one

place—does God say He modified His plan. His plan has been the same all along. That plan is for the power of the Holy Spirit to be present with the people of God. That's the bottom line and anyone who tells you anything different cannot back up their opinion from the Word of God. Yet we don't see this, so we have to make up rules of man, and exchange ideas about how and why miracles are so scarce among us today. Jesus told us right in this passage why we lack God's power.

Jesus used a very specific word to explain why He could only heal a few people. He identified that a lack of "honor" is what prevented great miracles from happening in Nazareth: "A prophet is not without *honor*, except in his hometown."

How in the world does honor play into miracles or the power of God being present with people? I believe it's because they could not see who He was, nor Who was empowering Him. They saw who He was through the lens of the past, as a boy they grew up with, but they could not see who He was in the present, and Who had descended upon Him at the River Jordan. Because they couldn't or wouldn't see this, He couldn't be who He truly was to them. The people of Nazareth saw Jesus as a son, a brother, a cousin, a devout neighbor boy. His hometown crowd and family missed healing, encouragement, and a touch from their Messiah because they did not honor Him.

So where does this leave *us*?

No doubt you believe in Jesus, right? Christians obviously believe in Jesus, but do you believe in the One He sent? His Holy Spirit? Do you believe in Him as much as you believe in Jesus? Because He *is* God. Jesus is our High Priest in bodily form sitting with the Father at this moment in time, and He's set to lead the Church, with the Holy Spirit, right now. Oftentimes we're good with Jesus and we're good with the Father, but we're not sure about the Holy Spirit. Yet He is the Spirit of Christ (Romans 8:9) and He was sent to Earth for us when Jesus ascended to His Father.

Does this not liken us to the people of Nazareth? Jesus could do no miracles because of the unbelief of the people. Think about this from a personal perspective: "Am I honoring the Holy Spirit today? Do I want Him?" Do you really want more of God? Do you have a strong desire to be filled with His Holy Spirit—a desire to work in power and to change lives? If your answer is yes, then I encourage you to open your heart to Him in faith and receive what I am trying to impart to you.

Let's look at another passage that shines a light on the meaning of the scriptures we have just read in Mark 6:

> [13] Now when Jesus came into the district of Caesarea Philippi, he asked his disciples, "Who do people say that the Son of Man is?" [14] And they said, "Some say John the Baptist, others say Elijah, and others Jeremiah or one of the prophets." [15] He said to them, "But who do you say that I am?" [16] Simon Peter replied, "You are the Christ, the Son of the living God." [17] And Jesus answered him, "Blessed are you, Simon Bar-Jonah! For flesh and blood has not revealed this to you, but my Father who is in heaven. [18] And I tell you, you are Peter, and on this rock I will build my church, and the gates of hell shall not prevail against it. [19] I will give you the keys of the kingdom of heaven, and whatever you bind on earth shall be bound in heaven, and whatever you loose on earth shall be loosed in heaven." Matthew 16:13-19

I have preached this passage on numerous occasions. I've

done Bible studies on it, written, prayed, and journaled about it. You're probably familiar with it because many scholars— including me—have come to believe it's about Jesus testing the disciples to see if they knew who He was. We couldn't be more wrong!

This passage is about *honor* and *blessing.* I want you to see this with your spiritual eyes.

Let's start with verses 13 and 14: "[13] Now when Jesus came into the district of Caesarea Philippi, he asked his disciples, "Who do people say that the Son of Man is?" [14] And they said, "Some say John the Baptist, others say Elijah, and others Jeremiah or one of the prophets."

Then Jesus asked them a really great question: "But who do *you* say that I am?" He's narrowing the expected answer down, isn't He? He's getting right to the core of the question. "So what about you?"

See, I always thought Jesus was testing these men. He's not. "[16] Simon Peter replied, 'You are the Christ, the Son of the living God.' [17] And Jesus answered him…" (take note of this word) "*Blessed* are you, Simon Bar-Jonah!" What was Jesus' intention in saying "Blessed are you" to Peter? To test him? No… to *bless* him. And Jesus wants to bless you too. He wants to bless every single one of us.

But *why* was Peter blessed? Don't miss this part— because Peter *honored* Jesus. Peter could just as easily have said, "Who do I think You are? You're my best friend. You are the most awesome teacher I have ever heard. You're a miracle worker." He could have picked many different things to describe Jesus and he would have been correct, but Peter picked the one thing that could *only* be said of Jesus.

He picked the one thing that honored Jesus the most: "You are the Christ, the Son of the living God."

I want you to take note of an important point: when Peter blessed the Lord, the Lord turned around and immediately blessed Peter. When Peter honored Jesus, Jesus immediately turned around and honored Peter.

Similarly, I believe, if Peter had said, "You are the best teacher I have ever heard," he would have received a different blessing. Peter's response gave Jesus the opening to bless Peter in equal measure (I'll prove this with scripture at the end of the chapter). If Peter had honored Jesus by calling Him a great teacher, Jesus would have given him a great teacher's blessing. If Peter had said, "You are my best friend," Jesus would have given him a best friend's blessing.

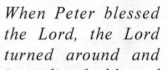

When Peter blessed the Lord, the Lord turned around and immediately blessed Peter.

But Peter called Him *the Christ*. He gave Jesus the greatest blessing that could ever be bestowed upon Him by a human being. In like measure, Peter received a great blessing from Jesus:

> [18] And I tell you, you are Peter, and on this rock I will build my church and the gates of hell shall not prevail against it. [19] I will give you the keys of the kingdom of heaven, and whatever you bind on earth shall be bound in heaven, and whatever you loose on earth shall be loosed in heaven. Matthew 16:18-19

This is not a prophet's blessing nor a teacher's blessing. This is a *Christ* blessing—only Jesus could have spoken with this authority concerning how His Church would be built. I'm willing to bet Peter is standing in Heaven saying, "Oh my, that blessing is continuing to expand across the face of the Earth, even today." How awesome is that?

Only Christ can command a Christ blessing. So we can see this passage is about honor and blessing and I believe with all of my heart you will receive the same measure of blessing you seek—the measure you offer up to Jesus. If you seek a worship blessing you will receive a worship blessing, but if you go seeking the Holy Spirit, you will receive a Holy Spirit blessing.

Measure for Measure

Whatever measure you use to honor the Lord is the same measure He'll use to bless you. This is a biblical principle.

Let me read it to you from a different angle in Luke 6:38: "Give, and it will be given to you. Good measure, pressed down, shaken together, running over, will be put into your lap. For with the measure you use it will be measured back to you." It's easy to recognize this scripture is about giving, but I want you to grasp the biblical principle at its core: "For *with the measure you use it will be measured back to you.*"

Honor the Holy Spirit. Come into God's presence and offer Him everything you have. *Submit* to whatever the Holy Spirit wants to do in your life. Hand over control. The issue most people struggle with, the real reason behind the limited honor we offer God, is our massive need. We come to the Lord with all this need but because of our theology and our intellect, because of past abuses or whatever we struggle with, we come to Him and say, "Lord, I honor You with this little portion I am able to offer."

To which God replies, "I love you but I am only able to bless you through this little portion of yourself you're offering to Me." He needs you to let your construct crumble, so you come to Him with all of your need, all your worship, and all of your being. God wants all of you, so when you give up your own way—when you fully submit your body, soul, and spirit, with arms open—you will receive.

Why is it like this? Jesus couldn't do miracles in Nazareth because the people *thought* they knew Him. As a result they had no idea how to truly honor Him, and the Spirit of God who empowered Him. Their keyhole was too small. They couldn't view Him as God, therefore they couldn't submit to Him nor the works of His Holy Spirit.

This doesn't have to be the case for you. I believe the Lord wants to pour out His power, not just upon us, but as a tsunami upon the whole Earth. I believe it. I pray and think about it all the time. I'm curious and I wonder about it. Yet I knock up against the wall and I ask, "Why? Lord, *why* do we not operate in Your full power?"

I believe we lack the miraculous because we lack sufficient honor toward the Holy Spirit.

Personal Prayer
Lord, I am so sorry for the limited honor I have offered You for so long. Teach me how to honor You Holy Spirit. I do not want to box You or limit You by my preconceived ideas of who You are. I admit now that I don't know and don't understand. I need You to reveal more to me from Your Word as to who You are. Please do not leave me in this state, help me to grow and know more of You. Thank you Lord for wanting this for me more than I want it.

Walking by the Holy Spirit
Chapter Eight

———⟨✦⟩———

In this chapter we will see what it means to live every aspect of one's life in the Holy Spirit. We've seen what it means to be *baptized* in the Holy Spirit, but what thoughts and principles would help us on a day-to-day basis after this? How does being baptized in the Holy Spirit help you approach Monday, Tuesday, and each day of every week?

As always, let's turn to God's Word for an answer to this question:

> [16] But I say, walk by the Spirit, and you will not gratify the desires of the flesh. [17] For the desires of the flesh are against the Spirit, and the desires of the Spirit are against the flesh, for these are opposed to each other, to keep you from doing the things you want to do. [18] But if you are led by the Spirit, you are not under the law. [19] Now the works of the flesh are evident: sexual immorality, impurity, sensuality, [20] idolatry, sorcery, enmity, strife, jealousy, fits of anger, rivalries, dissensions, divisions,

[21] envy, drunkenness, orgies, and things like these. I warn you, as I warned you before, that those who do such things will not inherit the kingdom of God. [22] But the fruit of the Spirit is love, joy, peace, patience, kindness, goodness, faithfulness, [23] gentleness, self-control; against such things there is no law. [24] And those who belong to Christ Jesus have crucified the flesh with its passions and desires. Galatians 5:16-24

In this passage we see several principles that will free you from the works of the flesh and unlock your ability to live life filled with the Holy Spirit. Paul tells us these principles come by *walking* in the Holy Spirit so the fruit we bear reflects who He is.

The Attributes of the Holy Spirit

Note that the nine characteristics of the fruit of the Spirit mentioned above are essentially a list of the Holy Spirit's attributes. These are not the attributes of the Church or of King David, and neither are these *your* natural attributes. Scripture tells us these nine attributes are "the fruit of the Spirit."

When you meet a person for the first time and you're trying to figure them out, the best way to do so is by spending time with them. Time will show you what they are like and who they are, revealing for example whether they're a nice person, a mean person, or somewhere in between. Only time in their company will uncover more of their personality traits, giving you insight into the way they live and act—the fruit they bear.

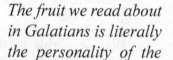

The fruit we read about in Galatians is literally the personality of the Holy Spirit

The fruit we read about in Galatians is literally the

personality of the Holy Spirit, and it's the reason we are supposed to spend more time in His presence. These can also be called the *attributes* of the Holy Spirit, and they reflect who He is. This is the personality of God expressed in the work of the Holy Spirit, and it's what separates Him from anybody else in the world, apart from Christ and the Father. What makes this so exciting is we have been given the opportunity to take on the personality of God through the Holy Spirit living inside of us. Bearing His fruit means we are being transformed into the image of Christ (2 Corinthians 3:18).

Another really important point we need to understand is God *designed* us to be led by the Holy Spirit. He is not an add-on—a bonus we receive now that we have Jesus. God didn't think, *It would be really great, after they receive Jesus, to give them a little bit of the Holy Spirit*. God's plan, before any man ever walked the Earth, was for you to be filled with the Holy Spirit; for you to take on the Holy Spirit's personality. You were made by God to be filled with and led by the Holy Spirit your entire life, and His plan goes beyond your earthly life—throughout eternity you will be led and filled by the Holy Spirit.

This aspect of how God created us may be challenging to you because you have a choice to be led or not be led by the Holy Spirit. Because God designed you to be led by the Holy Spirit, if you choose *not* to be led by Him, the reality of life on Earth is you open the door to being led by some other spirit. It might be a spirit of anger, a spirit of lust, or a spirit of envy—the influence of any spirit outside of the Holy Spirit, Jesus, and God the Father, will cause you to bear wicked fruit of the flesh.

The truth is it doesn't matter what you think or what you believe, God made you to be led by the Holy Spirit and when we reject the Holy Spirit we open ourselves to other kinds of (unholy) spirits. This is what's happening in our world today, and it's what separates Christians from non-Christians. Christian behavior tends to be judged more harshly, even by fellow believers. The only difference between a believer and a non-believer, however, is the Holy Spirit within the believer—that's all.

As Peter explained to the crowd on the day of Pentecost, "You will receive the gift of the Holy Spirit. [39] For the promise is for you and for your children and for all who are far off" (Acts 2:38b-39a). This mind-boggling Gift is what seals you as a believer in Jesus. The point that must not be missed is if you are *not* being led by the Holy Spirit then some other spirit is leading you. You *will* be ministered to, either by the Holy Spirit or by some other spirit, and personally, I certainly do not want to be led by any spirit other than the Holy Spirit.

Let me give you an example of this: let's say somebody betrayed you in the past, hurting you deeply but you have managed to overcome this betrayal. Down the road something similar happens and suddenly, you start experiencing those old emotions again. That old feeling of betrayal rises up within you so you start treating the person who has hurt you the second time the same the way you wish you had treated the person who first betrayed you. You put up walls and push back against the injustice, even though knowing in your heart it's not the scriptural thing to do. You may even start hating the individual who has wronged you. You push them away and think vengeful thoughts. Guess what? You're being ministered to by a spirit, and it is definitely not the Holy Spirit. You will be led by these spirits of impure emotion until you deny the carnal impulses they feed on, and make the Holy Spirit the Lord of your life. That's right—I said until you submit to the Spirit of Christ as the Lord of your life.

Do Not Miss the Grace of God

When you willingly accept His guidance, however, the nine attributes of the Holy Spirit will encompass and permeate every aspect of your life, enriching it beyond what you can imagine. Make no mistake, though, it is a battle, and Paul put this truth into the correct context: "For the desires of the flesh are against the Spirit, and the desires of the Spirit are against the flesh, for these are opposed to each other, to keep you from doing the things you want to do" (Galatians 5:17). When we resist the work of the Holy Spirit, we close the door to godly fruit, but as long as you're open and surrendering to the Holy Spirit, He will begin to bless *every* area of your life.

Sometimes we are also tempted to hold onto some carnal fruit, telling the Spirit of the Lord He can have this aspect of our life but not that one. This is where we lose our Spirit-led guidance and open the door to being ministered to by other spirits. Pay close attention here: *this is why it's an all-or-nothing type of deal.* These other spirits get a foothold and begin to take over because, as recipients of God's Spirit, when we refuse total surrender to Him what we're essentially doing is denying and rebelling against the Lordship of Jesus Christ. When we *withhold* areas of our life from the Holy Spirit, we enter into an implicit agreement to work with the enemy. At this point the enemy is permitted to suggest wicked thoughts for us to entertain: *That man hurt me so badly I am justified in hating him. I hope something bad happens to him as justice for the bad thing he did to me.* As soon as we choose to enter into this agreement against the Holy Spirit, an unforgiving spirit begins to work in our life.

There's a passage of scripture in Hebrews telling us to apply God's grace to others just as we receive it from Him: "See to it that no one fails to obtain the grace of God; that no 'root of bitterness' springs up and causes trouble, and by it many become defiled" (Hebrews 12:15). God's grace embodies the fact that He forgave you all your sins, which in turn means you have been given the grace (ability) to forgive those who sin against you.

When I refuse to forgive those who sin against me I become entangled in an agreement of my own making, to push against the will of God. Remember, the will of God is for me to be filled with the Holy Spirit. When there are areas of my life I have marked off by declaring to God, "I reserve the right to follow my own will in this regard," how can I be filled with the Holy Spirit?

Sadly, we choose to limit the Holy Spirit, whether it's to gratify sexual sin, alcoholism, bigotry, hatred, or deny the baptism, gifts, and works of the Holy Spirit in the Earth today. In many areas of life, sometimes knowingly or unknowingly, we choose to say, "I reserve the right to follow my own will in this." We must always seek to recognize when we have limited the Holy Spirit and then we must immediately repent of it.

Through repentance we open ourselves again to receive God's love, acceptance, and leading, enabling us to see the heart of God as opposed to seeing what the enemy desperately wants us to agree to. When we receive this revelation it strengthens us to use the name of Jesus to cut off these strongholds that bind us. We become emboldened to say, "I will not do that anymore," presenting the opportunity to replace rebellious, unscriptural thinking with God's truth.

God Wants You to Be Blessed Right Now

We must gain a deep revelation that God has blessed us while we're still on Earth right now. He has showered you with every spiritual blessing found in the heavenly places, as recorded in scripture: "Blessed be the God and Father of our Lord Jesus Christ, who has blessed us in Christ with every spiritual blessing in the heavenly places" (Ephesians 1:3). But you have to receive it.

This is a real eye-opener—it's not just for some who follow God closely. No, Paul is saying to the body of Christ, "You—*all of you who are filled with the Holy Spirit*—have access to and are blessed with every spiritual blessing in the heavenly places."

Have you ever wondered what Heaven is like? I have. I *do* sometimes wonder what Heaven is like and I wonder what it will feel like to be there. I wonder what it will be like when I first enter into Heaven and realize, *This is forever!* I wonder how much joy and peace I really will feel. I think it's important for us all to understand, it's the Holy Spirit who makes Heaven what it is. Heaven is filled with His

I think it's important for us all to understand, it's the Holy Spirit who makes Heaven what it is.

person—His fruit; it's who He is. His personality underpins the culture of Heaven!

This is why the Father promised you can have the Holy Spirit right now, because He wants the Kingdom of Heaven in your life while you still walk the Earth. Remember Jesus taught us to pray, "On Earth as it is in Heaven" (Matthew 6:10). He sent the Holy Spirit to live inside of you, thereby ensuring the Kingdom of Heaven has now come to Earth. Think about this—the actual soul and culture of Heaven is alive within you today!

That's precisely why Jesus had to leave and be with the Father. He said, "If I don't go then He (the Holy Spirit) won't come" (paraphrase of John 16:7). Jesus made it clear He wants you to have this monumental blessing and yet you're thinking, *Why don't I feel the culture of Heaven in my life?* Maybe the right question to ask is, "Am I absolutely 100% submitted to being filled with the Holy Spirit?" Only when you are totally submitted and committed will you be filled to the point where you clearly experience Heaven's culture. God has brought Heaven's culture right down to Earth to live inside of you, but it is your choice to be filled.

Listen to the words again: "Blessed be the God and Father of our Lord Jesus Christ, who has blessed us in Christ with every spiritual blessing in the heavenly places."

Can you imagine experiencing the fruit of the Holy Spirit to a degree beyond human understanding? Can you imagine love, joy, peace, patience, kindness, goodness, faithfulness, gentleness and self-control—every spiritual blessing in the heavenly places operating fully in your life as a direct download from Heaven into your spirit? When we get to Heaven it will be beyond anything we've ever understood or can even talk about here on Earth. We're just scraping the surface on Earth, but that same power and intensity is available to you today, right now, by God's design.

You Will Recognize Them by Their Fruits

This fruit of the Holy Spirit is the result of God living and being active within you—what I would call the evidence that salvation has actually occurred in your life. We trick ourselves sometimes by thinking, *I remember raising my hand and being saved. I remember saying the Lord's prayer of confession and receiving forgiveness. That prayer marks my salvation.*

I want to suggest we go back to what Jesus said, in which the evidence of salvation doesn't correspond with a time and place. The evidence of salvation revolves around whether or not *you* or *others* see the fruit of the Holy Spirit in your life. The challenge, of course, is this may go against some of the traditions of man—the dogma you've learned.

Listen to what Jesus said on this subject:

[15] "Beware of false prophets, who come to you in sheep's clothing but inwardly are ravenous wolves. [16] You will recognize them by their fruits. Are grapes gathered from thornbushes, or figs from thistles? [17] So, every healthy tree bears good fruit, but the diseased tree bears bad fruit. [18] A healthy tree cannot bear bad fruit, nor can a diseased tree bear good fruit. [19] Every tree that does not bear good fruit is cut down and thrown into the fire. [20] Thus you will recognize them by their fruits." Matthew 7:15-20

Jesus is talking about the fruit of the Holy Spirit in our lives. Please believe me when I say I know none of us is perfect. I do believe, however, that over a course of time it is imperative—it's critical—that you see these nine attributes growing in your life. If they're not growing in your life I would lovingly enquire, not in a judgmental way, but I would ask, "Why not?" Why are you not seeing the growth of these nine fruit in your life? Because if the Holy Spirit is in you, they *will* grow. Unless you're stiff-arming the Holy Spirit and saying, "No, I reserve the right to hold on to certain things in my life." Then they *won't* grow. And I'm not saying you aren't saved or you don't have the Holy Spirit living within you, but I will say it is very dangerous to resist the progression of the Holy Spirit's work, and His prompting to that end.

Do Not Quench the Spirit
No one on Earth can take these spiritual attributes from you, and I thank God for that. They can never be stolen but you can lose the sense of the attributes by quenching them in your life.

Paul tells the Church in 1 Thessalonians 5:19: "Do not quench the Spirit." What does he mean? To "quench" means to "extinguish," to "stifle" or "suppress." It really goes back to a previous point I made: when we willingly choose sin in our lives; when we willingly say, "Lord, I reserve the right to hold onto this," whatever that may be, we quench the manifest presence of the Holy Spirit in our lives.

The Holy Spirit still lives within us but we just can't feel Him, and His presence has little to no effect on our lives. In our humanity it is not easy to constantly be filled with the Holy Spirit. To be filled with the Holy Spirit means He has full access to my body—from the soles of my feet to the top of my head. He has full access to my spirit, soul (mind), will, and emotions—He has all of it. As He identifies places within me that continue to resist Him, I should be faithful then to say, "Lord, You're right and I repent of this resistance to Your Spirit. I confess my fault before You and I turn away from continuing this fleshly behavior, in submission to You."

When we are faithful in opening ourselves up to the

Holy Spirit, He fills up those areas that have previously resisted Him, and over time our capacity to hold the culture of Heaven expands. As this expansion continues, the fruit of these beautiful nine attributes of the Holy Spirit gain exponential momentum and power in our lives. So much so that the people around us begin to see His presence within us and they're touched by it—the witness of the Spirit within us ministers to them through us.

This is the desire of God's heart.

That's why Jesus said, "In the same way, let your light shine before others, so that they may see your good works and give glory to your Father who is in heaven" (Matthew 5:16). It is so important for us not to quench these attributes of Heaven's culture from flowing through us freely.

The Fruit of the Spirit Is a Walk into Simplicity
If you fellowship with Christians who say, "Oh, being a Spirit-filled Christian is so complex," my advice to you is to take a few steps back from those people, because God *has* made it simple. We follow Jesus. We devote ourselves to Him. We learn how to hear the voice of the Lord through scripture. We receive the Holy Spirit and He enables us to pursue things that are simple—we receive grace to perfect those things. In short, the fruit of the Spirit is a walk into the simplicity of the gospel.

This is where we enter into the peace God promises in His Word: "And the peace of God, which surpasses all understanding, will guard your hearts and your minds in Christ Jesus" (Philippians 4:7).

Spiritual Maturity
Growing in the fruit of the Spirit will move you from being

a spiritual child to a spiritual adult. I see this all the time—people who are still young in their faith want to make a mark for themselves and for the Lord. These people want to do something with their life and they want to leave a legacy for others. It's natural for them to want to make a mark—it's what sons and daughters do.

This mindset is often evident in young preachers and pastors—they want to make their mark on society. The marks

Growing in the fruit of the Spirit will move you from being a spiritual child to a spiritual adult.

they leave, however, are not always what they hoped for, and are sometimes difficult to erase. In contrast, spiritual parents and grandparents are not so interested in leaving a name for themselves. They're interested in *the name of Jesus being lifted up,* and that's the mark of a beautiful ministry. Spiritual maturity is the mark of a man or a woman who isn't interested in their own name being lifted up, but the mark of someone who would rather see the name of Jesus being lifted up.

Isn't it interesting that the Holy Spirit who brings the power of God to bear on humanity has never made a name for Himself, or mentioned Himself one time? The Holy Spirit is complete maturity, He wholly promotes Jesus and the Father, and as you mature in Him, so will you. Your ministry will not retain any self-promotion—what you have done or what others see about you. Your ministry will be about imparting into others the love of God for their benefit and for the glory of God.

What this spiritual maturity produces is the freedom to pour your life into other people, as opposed to constantly drawing from others to lift yourself higher. When the Spirit of the Lord is allowed to bear fruit within and through you, you will begin to move beyond spiritual immaturity.

Becoming spiritually mature is a beautiful place to be, and if there are specific sins in your life you are struggling to overcome, ask yourself if you have ever offered these sins up to the Lord? All it takes is saying:

> Lord I confess these sins before You (name each sin), and I ask You to give me the power (grace) to break every one of these recurring sins through the blood of Jesus Christ. Lord God I ask You to fill me to overflowing with the power that raised Jesus Christ from the dead. Fill me to overflowing so through the power of the Holy Spirit I can speak to these sins and declare them dead, moving forward in righteousness.

If you feel defeated in a specific area of your life, where you know within your spirit you have the ability to speak life into this area, I want to encourage you to accept the grace to move away from defeat. I pray you will ask the Holy Spirit to fill that very area of your life. Confess the sinful source of that defeat and ask for the power of God to become actively involved in delivering you from it.

Take Jesus' advice from John 16:23-24: "[23] In that day you will ask nothing of me. Truly, truly, I say to you, whatever you ask of the Father in my name, he will give it to you. [24] Until now you have asked nothing in my name. Ask, and you will receive, that your joy may be full."

Faith and the Gifts of the Holy Spirit
Chapter Nine

In Paul's first letter to the Corinthians we find an interesting passage referring to the gifts of the Holy Spirit: "⁴Now there are varieties of gifts, but the same Spirit; ⁵and there are varieties of service, but the same Lord; ⁶and there are varieties of activities, but it is the same God who empowers them all in everyone" (1 Corinthians 12:4-6).

What I conclude from this passage is that these gifts of God are available right now and they are distributed to *all* believers, not just a select few. In fact, if you have made a profession of faith in Jesus Christ you have already received a portion of these gifts. This scripture does *not* refer to talents or past experiences, although talents and prior experience will almost certainly have helped you in developing the capacity to express your spiritual gifts. The simple truth is you have been blessed with at least one God-given,

Faith is the base necessary to receiving spiritual gifts.

miraculous gift. We will focus on "miraculous gifting" in another chapter, but I first want to mention what is perhaps the most important foundation these gifts are based upon: that foundation is *faith*.

Faith is the base necessary to receiving spiritual gifts. Faith is in fact the foundation to every aspect of our relationship with God, especially when it relates to the Holy Spirit. This means specifically in relation to the spiritual gifts we are meant to use within the Body of Christ.

To properly understand the essence of faith, we'll first focus on faith, then turn our attention to the functionality of the gifts so we have a better understanding of both subjects.

Let's begin by asking ourselves four questions. While the first three questions are critical to your general walk with God, the fourth question will be the springboard to understanding why faith is necessary, and how it influences your interaction with the Holy Spirit and His gifts:

1: Do you believe the Bible is God's Word?

2: Do you believe God's Word is complete truth?

3: Do you believe God's Word is complete truth for you?

These are critical questions for all Christians to answer. Your faith won't take you very far if you did not answer "Yes" to each of these questions. The fourth question may seem strange but I believe the Holy Spirit asks this question to lay the foundation of our walk with God. The question is:

4: Do I need faith in my life?

If your response to this question is to think, *What?*

Are you kidding me? We're Christians! Of course faith is necessary in our lives, then let me tell you there are plenty of Christians who by their actions show they believe they don't need faith in their life. They live their lives based upon their five senses: what they can see, hear, taste, smell, and feel. There are millions of believers who have journeyed to the edge of their beliefs, their intellect, and their theology, yet at that place where faith is supposed to emerge—a place beyond the five senses—they stop short of engaging in faith. Instead they continue to make spiritual decisions based on their five senses.

Now don't get me wrong, our five senses are God-given and are meant to help us navigate the natural world, but God never intended our five senses to lead us when making spiritual decisions. This is where faith is meant to be employed. That's why I believe it's important to ask these questions, "Do you believe the Bible is God's Word? Do you believe the Word of God is true, and do you believe the Word of God is the ultimate truth you should adhere to in your own life?"

If your answer to all these questions was "Yes," then you are perfectly positioned to engage the realm of faith. This is where you step across the edge separating our physical world from the spiritual realm. When you step into this spiritual realm of faith, it will take you further than you could ever journey in the natural world. Even though we are able to accomplish a lot in the natural world, we risk making our own goals our life's focus instead of obeying God's leading.

What I mean by this is there are plenty of astoundingly large churches, many of which have lots of great programs with good movement in them. Also, there are very inspiring people in our world; is it possible that some well-intended ministries have resorted to accomplishing these things with their five senses? I don't want to be one of them. I want to be a man who walks by faith, because scripture says without faith it's impossible to please God (paraphrase of Hebrews 11:6).

Is it possible for me to do great things that benefit God's Kingdom but because they are done in the natural, using my five senses, God is not pleased? Yes! It certainly is, because if I can apply myself to a problem and with my ingenuity figure out a way around it or through it, I may point back to my accomplishment and say, "Look at how I overcame this problem." Whereas God may look at it and say, "I'm not pleased. This is not the solution I wanted."

Faith Is What You Do

I think the faith of many Christians is shipwrecked when they come up against the supernatural. Many church people fear the supernatural, but it's because they don't understand faith. It's faith that takes us into the realm of the supernatural. Faith takes us beyond that place where we don't have the security of an answer. When your faith is based upon the Word of God, it gives you the confidence and courage to step out, move forward, and to go beyond the comfort zone of your current theology. It's like standing on the edge of a canyon knowing you must reach the other side, yet recognizing you don't have the resources to get there.

Standing on the edge we think, *I can't jump that far, and I don't know how to fly. I can't translate myself there so I have no way of crossing this chasm...* and then the Spirit says, "Take a step." To which the natural mind replies, *But I will fall!* Now this is where faith comes in. When your mind tells you, *If I take a step I will fall*, it's because you're looking at it with your senses.

In contrast, faith takes us to the place where we look at things that seem impossible in the flesh, but in the spiritual realm we know we are being prompted to "Take a step. Just one step..." Simply stated, faith is not what you believe; faith is what you *do*. We get that mixed up in our church circles where we say, "Well my faith says..." Don't tell me what your faith says, let me see your life and I'll tell you what you believe. *Faith is what you do.*

> *Simply stated, faith is not what you believe; faith is what you do.*

I believe our faith has a significant bearing on what we do with the gifts of the Holy Spirit. The reason for this is because the gifts cannot be interpreted by our five senses—they don't make sense to the natural mind, to the eye of the world looking in. Yet God instituted the gifts of the Spirit, and this is where our focus should be.

The Church needs gifts because they force us to go to the edge of our senses and by faith trust God that His system is at work. We need these spiritual gifts, and we need them more desperately than most people realize. It is by faith I say we must make space for the gifts in our lives. By faith we have to say, "We must make room for gifts in the local church."

The Gifts of the Spirit and the Personality of Jesus

There are three different sets of spiritual gifts but for the purpose of this book I will present only the first set. I have already established the foundation for this first set of gifts by revealing the importance of the fruit of the Spirit. Just as we recognize the fruit of the Spirit—love, joy, peace, patience, kindness, goodness, faithfulness, gentleness, and self-control—being the persona of the Holy Spirit, so this next set of gifts relate to the persona of Jesus Christ.

This fruit starts becoming active in a person's life when the individual accepts Jesus as his or her Savior, and the Holy Spirit enters in. The Spirit then begins rooting out everything not part of the destiny God has for you. He keeps that which is part of who God intended you to be, and He replaces the rest with His persona, with His personality. This is what it means to be filled with the Holy Spirit—the evidence of this infilling is the fruit of the Holy Spirit becoming recognizable in a person's life.

I believe this first set of five gifts I'm about to present to you identifies the personality of Jesus Christ, just as the fruit of the Spirit identifies the personality of the Holy Spirit. You may not have heard it put this way before but I will refer you to the gospels and some other New Testament passages revealing the personality of Jesus Christ. I will also share with you a passage of scripture from Romans 12:4-5, which refers to believers being "one body in Christ."

If we truly are the Body of Christ then the functionality of Jesus while He walked on Earth will be the same functionality we have in the local church. The things Jesus did are the things we should do. He did not redo His program to fit our human limitations. As a matter of fact, His program is affirmed in the book of Romans where it clearly states that you and I *are* the body of Christ.

In the next chapter we will explore in more detail the specific gifts given to the Body of Christ; gifts exemplified and provided by Christ Himself, the Head of the Body.

Before you go on, stop, let's take a moment to pray for wisdom and understanding.

✶ ✶ ✶

Personal Prayer
Lord, separate from our thoughtful investigation any personal preference that would give us unhealthy allowance to agree or disagree. Let us see truth and truth only that we might have all that You want us to have.

The Five-fold Gifts
to the Church

For the Church—the Body of Christ—to function the way Jesus did when He walked the Earth it makes sense that we would need to be equipped with the gifts Jesus had, would you agree? Did you know that scripture lists the gifts Christ gave to His Church *and* the explicit reason the gifts were granted?

> "¹¹ Now these are the gifts Christ gave to the church: the apostles, the prophets, the evangelists, and the pastors and teachers. ¹² Their responsibility is to equip God's people to do his work and build up the church, the body of Christ." Ephesians 4:11-12 (NLT)

Take close note that this passage clearly reveals the purpose of these gifts: to prepare people to do the work of the Kingdom, and to build the Kingdom—a clear and simple objective.

As mentioned in the last chapter, I present to you that what this set of five gifts reflects is nothing less than the personality of Jesus Christ. I have heard Dr. Clem Ferris teach many times that all the work Jesus ever did, and everything He ever said throughout the gospels, was ultimately funneled through one or more of these five areas. Since these personality traits lived out by Jesus are identified for us in the above scripture, let's go through them:

Apostle: The writer of Hebrews called Jesus our apostle and high priest, "Therefore, holy brothers, you who share in a heavenly calling, consider Jesus, the apostle and high priest of our confession" (Hebrews 3:1).

Prophet: In the book of Deuteronomy, Moses makes a prophetic statement about Jesus the prophet, "The Lord your God will raise up a prophet like me from among you, from your brothers—it is to Him you shall listen" (Deuteronomy 18:15).

Evangelist: Jesus' heart to share the good news was made known when he said, "The Spirit of the Lord is upon me because He has anointed me to proclaim good news to the poor" (Luke 4:18a).

Pastor: When questioned by Pharisees regarding His works Jesus said, "I am the good shepherd. The good shepherd lays down his life for the sheep" (John 10:11).

Teacher: Even the Pharisees acknowledged Jesus as a teacher when they tried to trap Him: "And they sent their disciples to Him along with the Herodian saying, 'Teacher, we know that you are true and teach the way of God truthfully, and you do not care about anyone's opinion, for you are not swayed by appearances'" (Matthew 22:16).

Paul was led by the Spirit when writing to the Ephesians because he accurately described the personality of Jesus.

Jesus not only lived these attributes, He *was and still is* these very attributes.

People sometimes say, "I wish I knew what Jesus was like; what His demeanor was." If you want to know what Jesus is like, view Him through the gospel. Just look through the lens of these five qualities. These attributes reveal the personality of Jesus, and if we—the Body of Christ—are submitted to the Holy Spirit, the Holy Spirit will raise these gifts up in our midst so we see the

People sometimes say, "I wish I knew what Jesus was like; what His demeanor was."

Body of Christ in each other. That's His plan and what He wants us to do, but so many people deny the gifts given to us these days.

There are entire denominations built upon denying the gifts, yet when you deny the gifts you deny the Body of Christ. How can a church function when the people in that church deny the gifts, thereby denying Christ? The result is a church based upon the five senses, and that church *will not* please the Lord. No one will please the Lord if their life is based strictly upon the five senses because this doesn't require any faith, and as we saw in a previous chapter, without faith it is impossible to please God (Hebrews 11:6). We are the Body of Christ, so we must function the way Jesus functioned. We must see what Jesus saw, and we must minister the way Jesus did, just as He asked us to.

The Function of the Gifts

In order to use these gifts to effectively equip God's people to do His work and build up the Church, we must first understand their function, and how they should be applied. We need to distinguish whether all the gifts are intended for every believer or if some are best suited to certain members of the Body. All five gifts or offices of ministry are not given to every believer, and a short analysis of each gift will help determine to which members of the Body of Christ they are best suited.

The role of apostles is to build the kingdom of God. That's what they spend their time thinking about and what they envision. In modern times, apostles are sometimes called missionaries but they are so much more. Some pastors are apostles, who, in their heart just want to equip people and send them out to build the Kingdom. That's a good thing because in the absence of this aspect of the Body of Christ, the local church would just get fat and content without any distribution into the community. We would close the doors and require a password to gain access—while the thought of this might make you smile, it's a hard truth we must face. The end result of our churches would be a range of safe havens—places that would be all about *us*.

God, however, puts the desire in some people to get out there and build the Kingdom. They have a drive to reach into the marketplace, to go to Guatemala, to Mexico, and to Haiti, to take the Kingdom beyond our borders and to plant churches in all the world. That's what an apostle does.

Then there are prophets. These are the individuals who earnestly want to hear the voice of God. We hear God as He speaks to us individually through scripture, into our spirit, but a prophet speaks God's Word to us as a congregation. What the prophet does is keep us tied to the Word of God. They keep us trusting the Word of God by exhortation inspired by the Holy Spirit.

We must understand the Church is at risk of taking our eyes off the Word of God—to become program driven and program led. This is not God's will for the Church. The beginning of 1 Corinthians 14 tells us that the role of the prophet, or the role of prophecy in the local church is to build up, to comfort, and to encourage (exhort) the Church. These qualities are seriously needed in the Body of Christ today.

The evangelist feels deeply for every unsaved person they meet. They see a vast harvest of people as lost, desperately needing someone to tell them about God's love and grace that is found in receiving the good news of Jesus Christ. The role of the evangelist is extremely important to the local church as the people they lead to salvation are directed to a local church for spiritual guidance and formation—to discover their place and gifts in the Body of Christ.

The need for pastors is probably the most evident role in the local church. Caring for, shepherding, equipping the flock, and binding up the broken-hearted, are crucial requirements for all local churches. The most likely place people will discover and develop their gift is in a local church, under the guidance of their pastor.

The teacher is critical in maintaining the accuracy and integrity of the Word of God. A teacher's role in the church is not only to examine, analyze, and investigate scripture for meaning and context, but also to lead and encourage the members to study the Word for themselves. A teacher also inspires deeper insight and revelation into the Word.

All five gifts or offices are extremely important in the Body of Christ, as all five are dimensions of Jesus and they must be embraced in the local Body. I would go so far as to say, if any one of these aspects are removed from the local church it becomes a chapel and no longer exists as a *church*. What we call these gifts is less important than their application, but I want to suggest we should honor what scripture calls them.

It is important to note that it's not what *you* say that legitimizes and gives credibility to the gift in you, it's what other people see operating in you and in your life. You must therefore put yourself in a position where your gift is being used in the local church. Many members sit in church watching the Body of Christ all around them, and they've never stepped forward to serve in any capacity.

You have been given a gift by God Himself, and it's as much a part of you as your personality is. You will never be satisfied as a human being on this Earth until you embrace it, even if you barely understand it right now. This is where faith comes in but remember, exercising faith isn't what you *say*, exercising faith is what you *do*. I want to challenge you today to step out in faith and discover what God has for you.

Levels of Expression
Something that needs to be understood is these five gifts are expressed on various levels in the church, across the world. To illustrate this, I will use an example from that second group of gifts mentioned earlier that we're not discussing here (known as the Ministry of Helps). The first level of expression of a gift is really just between you and someone else. For example, when somebody shakes your hand as you walk into church and you feel, *Wow, that person really knows how to make someone feel at home... I feel deeply welcomed by this person.*

Some of us rush in so fast we don't even notice the

person shaking our hand. Stop and recognize the person shaking your hand. They are welcoming you into the house of God—that's the gift of hospitality. The gift may only be for those in the immediate community they can touch, but it's a good thing because most gifts in the Body of Christ are personal. They're designed for you and who you can touch on a regular, limited basis.

The second level of gifts moves from a personal touch to something that's recognized in the entire Body of Christ. It's not so much about you but rather others seeing and recognizing that God has touched you with a special grace—an anointing, or the filling of a gift that you use to serve or equip the *global* Body of Christ.

A myth I hear in the church is that unless you are doing something for the church globally, you have not risen to the level God wants you to reach. I don't believe this is true at all. I believe God gives gifts to people based upon the destiny He spoke over each individual in their mother's womb. You may only ever touch someone by shaking hands outside, or sorting and counting the tithes and offerings after services on a weekend, but it's an absolute blessing to the church, and it's the gift of service you have been given by your Creator. You may also be the person who causes the next Billy Graham to come back to church the following Sunday, where they are saved.

This church-wide anointing is served inside the local church, but then there is also a wider scope of anointing that occurs regionally. Some individuals prayerfully and faithfully walk out a journey of developing a supportive ministry, and members from other churches begin to attend and be equipped by this ministry, so it begins touching people regionally. That's another logical level of anointing; when other churches look in and say, "We see this anointing and it's a value to our Body. There's a gift-set working there, and we want to engage with it." God may take it further, but at that point it's regional.

So we have one-to-one impact, we have church-wide impact, we have regional impact, and logically it goes further to a national impact where gifts flow on a national level.

Then there is also a worldwide impact where people take teams to Mexico, Haiti, Cuba, Guatemala, and other countries on different continents all over the world. So even inside a local church there are various levels of gifting recognized within that church but also by others around the world who are touched by that same gift. Mark Tubbs describes these levels of anointing in his book, *Relational Transformation.*[14]

Recognizing Your Gift

If no gift has been revealed in you yet, you might be wondering if you even have a gift. Well, let me settle that for you—scripture says you *do* have a gift, and maybe more than one. "Well I don't know what my gift is," you might say. The fact is you don't really have to know what your gift is at this point. What you need to do is continue submitting to the Holy Spirit as we discussed in earlier chapters. Submit to the Holy Spirit, let the fruit of the Holy Spirit fill you, and you will begin to move toward an understanding of your gift.

Allow me to provide a few thoughts for you to consider that I think will help you recognize the gift you have received. When you attend a service, while you're sitting there, if your predominant thought is, *I want to know where this church is going. What's our goal, where are we headed? Are we reaching out to our community? Is the Kingdom of God being built? Which ministries here are spreading into the region?* If these are your thoughts, you're probably apostolic.

If, however, you're sitting there thinking, *This congregation needs a Word from the Lord! Lord, I pray that today we will hear from You.* Perhaps you sense a message in your heart that you somehow just know the church needs. You might simply see somebody and just know that person needs a Word from the Lord. If these are your dominant thoughts, chances are you're prophetic.

If you're upset with the pastor because he doesn't give an invitation to accept Jesus as Savior at the end of every service, chances are, you're an evangelist! You're all upset, thinking, *People need Jesus, isn't that what it's all about?* Praise God for your frustration because that's how God wired you and it's what the church needs.

If you're looking around at everyone in the church thinking, *Man, are we caring for people? Look at that person, they're hurting, they're struggling... do we have the ministry capability here to walk with them, to help them get better and to build them up so they can function in their family? How is their family?* If these are your thoughts, you think like a pastor.

If, while taking notes during the pastor's message you believe the pastor missed or wasn't able to adequately convey a critical point in the message, or you believe they perhaps didn't fully grasp the depth of another point and you send a ten page email citing scripture with supporting commentary... you're probably a teacher.

These are the dimensions of Jesus—His personality. This is what He placed inside His Body, the local church.

It's who He is and how He operated on Earth—as an apostle, as a prophet, as an evangelist, as a pastor, and as a teacher. As Paul said in Ephesians 4:11, He also gave to the Church apostles and prophets, pastors, evangelists, and teachers.

So what I'm saying is your church and the whole Body of Christ needs you, and it all goes back to faith. You're either going to rely upon your natural senses or you're going to have to begin exercising your faith. You may say, "Yeah, yeah, yeah, I'm glad there are gifts in the church, but that's not for me. I'd rather walk away and leave those people who operate in the gifts to do what they do—as long as it doesn't get too weird! As for me, I'll just continue doing what I've been doing." I want to remind you, without faith it's impossible to please God.

This means if you haven't used the gift God has given to you, you have no idea of the level of anointing you have. Don't let the word "anointing" scare you—a king was anointed in the Old Testament as a symbol of the presence of the Holy Spirit resting upon them. It simply means it's the level of infilling, the level of grace, the intended impact of the Spirit-empowered gift He's placed inside you.

Allow me to illustrate what this means. Think about the shower you have in your home. It has a hot water tank that sends water through the pipes, which flows out through the shower head. The shower head represents the gift in the Body of Christ. What happens in some churches today is we spend time looking at the different shower heads saying, "Look how shiny it is and all the different directions the box says it can send water! Look how wide the spread is supposed to be," but the bottom line is the shower head is pointless without the water being turned on! The water is the

106

fruit of the Spirit as far as the shower is concerned, and I find many people focus on the shower head when it does nothing without the fruit of the Spirit flowing through it, touching others.

So my counsel to you is, if you'll spend time getting the water hot—that means spending time with the Holy Spirit and allowing Him to work *in* you by faith—this hot water can't help but come through the shower head once it's turned on. *You* have to turn it on, though, and God has given you all the resources to make it happen. He's put the hot water inside you, He's put the shower head inside you, He has given you the faucet handle, but it's up to you to activate it. This is because faith isn't what you *believe,* faith is what you *do* with what you believe (James 2:14-26).

Faith isn't what you believe, faith is what you do with what you believe

It is *all* about Jesus. It's about us as the Body of Christ serving Him by walking in mutual respect with each other in terms of the various gifts we have. It's not about trying to compare gifts or being envious of the gifts of others, but humbly and gently walking forward with the understanding that as Jesus was, so are we! It's His Body, it's His life, and they are His Words we live out with each other. *That's* the fruit of the Holy Spirit—the Spirit of Christ.

So I'm asking you to engage today, engage, and see what the Lord will do. I pray the Lord will raise up the gifts in you and that if you don't know what your spiritual gift is, the Lord would reveal it to you.

Personal Prayer
Lord, how have You made us? We want to know so we can fulfill the roles given to us at salvation. The gifts are real, I declare it today to You, the One who gave them to me. I choose to honor Your gifts. Thank you Lord for the exciting opportunity to be a part of the building of your Kingdom.

Conclusion
Chapter Eleven

———◦∭∭◦———

Thank you for reading through all the chapters. It really blesses me you took the time and effort to at least give the material a chance. I pray what I wrote and demonstrated with scripture resonates in your heart. I pray you now grasp and fully understand how crucial it is to be *filled* with the Holy Spirit. And I pray you now have insight into how important it is that you go further with the Holy Spirit because you want to. Hopefully I've sufficiently "de-weirded" everything related to the Holy Spirit.

If you struggled to see what this would look like in your life or ministry, then this conclusion will bless you. I have summarized all the chapters, highlighting the concepts I believe crucial to the book and to the necessity of your infilling. Hopefully you now understand how desperate our *need* for the Holy Spirit is. Even more than that, our world *needs* the Holy Spirit in you, and you *need* the Holy Spirit to navigate evangelizing the world.

Which brings us back to the reason for this book:

evangelism. By now you should realize you cannot complete your commission without the power of the Holy Spirit. Don't waste a lifetime trying. The Holy Spirit will always break out of every container you try to box Him into. Submit to God and allow His Spirit to take control.

By now you should have read and understood enough scripture to—at the very least—theologically understand that this material is not "of the devil." Instead, you should see and understand the perfect algorithm for New Covenant ministry in the book of Acts. As I have mentioned already, the Holy Spirit fell and the early Church did the acts. You will never find the full power of God in programming. The *presence* of God brings the power of God.

Let us now take a look at the summary of chapters:

Chapter 1: Salvation

Salvation is truly the most important message for the New Testament Church, but we need to have ears to hear the Holy Spirit to claim the full benefits of salvation. When I refer to salvation, I'm not talking about what we *think* we understand about salvation, but rather what the scriptural term really means. Salvation means we have received *everything* Christ has to offer us in this life, but we need to appropriate it.

A key to understanding the baptism of the Holy Spirit is to recognize the disciples' shift from Old Testament saints to New Testament saints at the resurrection of Jesus Christ. This is when the new covenant is established.

Chapter 2: The Second Baptism

There are two infillings of the Holy Spirit—one is involuntary at salvation, and one *completely* voluntary. There is a difference between *receiving* the Holy Spirit when you

110

accept Jesus as your Savior (scripture is very clear about this), and what happens when you are *filled* with the Holy Spirit when you specifically seek God for this baptism.

In this second instance, you have to be ready and hungry to be filled with the Holy Spirit; you must have a strong desire to be filled, and most importantly, you must *ask* to be filled. You have to *want* the anointing of the Holy Spirit.

Chapter 3: The Baptism of the Holy Spirit

Baptism into the Holy Spirit is a baptism into *power.* Jesus told us this from the beginning. We are also not to be led by an inferior, ungodly spirit. If we fail to be led by the Holy Spirit, however, this becomes inevitable.

In church, we often feel it's the pastor, the platform, or the teaching that lights the world. Yes, the anointing and the power of the Holy Spirit comes in through the pastor but he's not the one who lights up *the community. You* are! And bear in mind, the Holy Spirit is always ready, but we're usually not. We need to *get* ready.

One of our underlying themes is reflected in that the Holy Spirit did not limit what Stephen or Phillip could accomplish. We, therefore, should not put Him in a box by trying to limit His call and anointing on others' lives. This is because every one of us, including you, have been destined to fulfill this call before birth. Consider *you* have a destiny that was spoken over you in your mother's womb by Almighty God, and *this destiny is unleashed through the baptism of the Holy Spirit.*

Chapter 4: Receive the Holy Spirit

When the apostles heard that Samaria had received the Word of God, we saw the word "received" is written in the original Greek as *dechomai.* This is a passive verb that indicates a welcome reception of whatever is being offered. The literal meaning is "to receive with *ready reception* what is offered[15]."

When they "received" the Holy Spirit, however, in verses 15 and 17 of Acts 8, the Greek word here is *lambano,* which is an active aggressive verb, suggesting a self-prompted taking. The literal definition of *lambano* means: "to take, lay hold of; to receive[16]." This means we are to actively seek and lay hold of the baptism in the Holy Spirit.

Further, apart from the Holy Spirit's indwelling, there is a baptism into the *power and fire* of the Holy Spirit. The Holy Spirit lives within the believer but that doesn't mean we are always filled with His presence. This is evident by the frequent works of our flesh. We are to have an ongoing hunger and desire for the infilling of the Holy Spirit, with a subsequent ongoing infilling, or refilling of His presence, if you will.

Chapter 5: Refilled with the Holy Spirit
Evangelism and boldness were a result of the infilling of the Holy Spirit in the early Church, but it came in great measure when using the boldness and authority as empowered by the Holy Spirit.

All those at the prayer meeting in Acts 4:31 were *refilled* with the Holy Spirit. This took place less than a year after the infilling at Pentecost. It demonstrates the infilling of the Spirit was not a one-time event. This means the Holy Spirit is telling us it's a good thing to be *continuously* filled with the Holy Spirit.

The third point I make in this chapter is after you are baptized in the name of Jesus it is *imperative* that you are baptized in the Holy Spirit. This is because you will not be able to minister in power without Him, and the world responds mostly to His power.

More than power, being filled with the Holy Spirit means having access to the fruit of the Spirit: love, joy, peace, patience, kindness, goodness, faithfulness, gentleness, and self-control (Galatians 5:22-23). We are therefore filled with this fruit of the Holy Spirit, which are spiritual manifestations not natural within our human nature.

In Acts, Phillip, who had at this point become an evangelist, took the Word of God (salvation) to the Samaritans but Peter and John took the baptism of the Holy Spirit because "[16] he had not yet fallen on any of them, but they had only been baptized in the name of the Lord Jesus. [17] Then they laid their hands on them and they received the Holy Spirit" (Acts 8:12-17). Again we see evidence of two separate infillings but also that the Holy Spirit wanted these new believers to be *filled* with His Spirit so they could start transforming others.

Lastly, I believe water baptism should precede the baptism of the Holy Spirit.

Chapter 6: Three Baptisms
In this chapter we looked at the three distinct baptisms, and their respective significance:

The Baptism of Blood: This is the first baptism we encounter in scripture. At the moment you're saved, when your spirit is sealed by the Holy Spirit until the day of redemption, you are baptized in the blood of Jesus. (Death of sin.)

The Baptism of Water: The second baptism is the baptism of water, symbolizing our death and resurrection with Jesus Christ into new life. This is an act of obedience. (Death of the will.)

The Baptism with the Holy Spirit: This baptism provides the power to remove all flesh-life in you. To remove anything you can lay claim to, you must be drowned in the Holy Spirit, and filled with the Holy Spirit. (Death of fear.)

This is so important yet it is the threshold at which so many people stop moving forward in being baptized in the Holy Spirit. Fear keeps them frozen, masked by religion, theology, and insufficient teaching.

Faith is what grasps all three baptisms.

Faith is what grasps all three baptisms.

Chapter 7: Honor the Holy Spirit

Jesus could do no mighty work in His hometown because "A prophet is not without honor, except in his hometown and among his relatives and in his own household" (Mark 6:4). Jesus used this very specific word, "honor," for a reason. It is my belief that the reason we see so little power in the Church today is because we fail to honor the Holy Spirit. This is a very grievous offense to God, and the results are evident on the Earth.

Peter honored Jesus as the Messiah. In return, Peter received an astonishing blessing from the Messiah. Had he honored Jesus as his best friend, he would have received a best friend's blessing. This shows us we are to honor the Holy Spirit because the measure you use to honor the Lord is the same measure He'll use to bless you. This is a biblical

114

principle (Matthew 7:2).

Honor and submit to God the Holy Spirit, hand over control in your life and you will not lack power in your life and ministry.

Chapter 8: Walking by the Holy Spirit

We saw from Galatians 5:16-24 that the fruit of the Holy Spirit is equivalent to the attributes of the Holy Spirit, which are love, joy, peace, patience, kindness, goodness, faithfulness, gentleness, self-control. Paul tells us these attributes are grown in us by *walking* in the Holy Spirit so the fruit we bear reflects who He is. This means the only difference between a believer and a non-believer is the Holy Spirit within the believer. This fruit of the Holy Spirit is the result of God living and being active within you—what I would call the evidence that salvation has actually occurred in your life.

When there are areas of your life you have marked off by declaring to God, "I reserve the right to follow my own will in this regard," how can you be filled with the Holy Spirit? He sent the Holy Spirit to live inside of you, thereby ensuring the Kingdom of Heaven has now come to Earth. The soul and culture of Heaven is alive within you today! He wants the Kingdom of Heaven manifested in your life while you still walk the Earth. You are blessed right now, and seated in Heavenly places. Submit all areas of your life to Him completely to enjoy this fullness of grace.

Do not miss this grace of God! God's grace embodies the fact that He forgave you all your sins, which in turn means you have been given the grace (ability) to forgive those who sin against you. In the same way, do not quench the Spirit! No one on Earth can take these spiritual attributes from you but you can lose the sense of the Spirit's attributes by quenching them in your life.

To "quench" means to "extinguish," to "stifle" or "suppress." When we willingly choose sin in our lives; when we willingly say, "Lord, I reserve the right to hold onto this," whatever it may be, we quench the manifest presence of the Spirit in our lives.

Spiritual maturity, in contrast, is growing in the fruit of the Spirit. This growth produces the freedom to pour your life into other people, as opposed to constantly drawing from others to lift yourself higher. This empowers you to fulfill your call and win more souls to Christ.

Chapter 9: Faith and the Gifts of the Holy Spirit

These gifts of God are critical to accomplish the Great Commission—they are available right now and are distributed to *all* believers, not just a select few. *Faith* is the base necessary to receiving spiritual gifts.

If you've made a profession of faith in Jesus Christ you have already received a portion of these gifts. Our five senses are God-given and are meant to help us navigate the natural world, but God never intended our five senses to lead us when making spiritual decisions. This is where *faith* is meant to be employed.

Faith takes hold of (appropriates) these spiritual gifts, and we saw in the book of James that faith is not what you *believe,* but rather faith is what you *do.*

Chapter 10: The Five-fold Gifts to the Church

For the Church—the Body of Christ—to function the way Jesus did when He walked the Earth, it makes sense that we would need to be equipped with the gifts Jesus had and oper-ated in: Apostle, Prophet, Evangelist, Pastor, and Teacher. It is worth noting that Jesus not only lived these attributes, He *was* these very attributes.

Just as we recognize the fruit of the Spirit—love, joy, peace, patience, kindness, goodness, faithfulness, gentleness, and self-control—being the persona of the Holy Spirit, so this set of gifts relate to the persona of Jesus Christ.

The role of the *apostle* is to build the Kingdom of God.

The *prophet* earnestly wants to hear the voice of God. He or she keeps us tied to the Word of God, and trusting the Word of God by exhortation inspired by the Holy Spirit.

The *evangelist* feels deeply for every unsaved person they meet. They see a vast harvest of people as lost, desperately needing someone to tell them about God's love and grace that is found in the good news of Jesus Christ. The role of the evangelist is extremely important to the local church as the people they lead to salvation are directed to a local church for spiritual guidance and discipleship—to discover their place and gifts in the Body of Christ.

The *pastor* cares for, shepherds, and equips the flock, as well as binding up the broken-hearted. This ministry is a crucial requirement for all local churches. The most likely place people will discover and develop their gift is in a local church, under the guidance of their pastor.

The *teacher* maintains the accuracy and integrity of the Word of God. A teacher's role in the church is not only to examine, analyze, and investigate scripture for meaning and context, but also to lead and encourage the members to study the Word for themselves. A teacher also inspires deeper insight and revelation into the Word.

All five gifts or offices are extremely important in the Body of Christ, as all five are dimensions of Jesus and they must be embraced in the local Body.

It is important to note that it's not what *you* say that legitimizes and gives credibility to the gift in you, it's what other people see operating in you and in your life.

Take time to discover and recognize your gift. Then begin to use it!

In Closing

Never forget that evangelism is the primary reason for the baptism of the Holy Spirit. He will empower you to share your immensely powerful gifts with others, so they can be seated in heavenly places with Jesus too. So they can be saved from the unthinkable.

When you apply the principles in this book you should naturally start either going out yourself, or sending people out with the gospel in a beautiful New Testament way. When you *need* the Holy Spirit—when you realize how desperate we really are without His continuous infilling—He will be able to fill you. Then you will experience the power the early Church walked in, and no religious dogma on Earth can rob you of receiving an encounter with Almighty God.

The apostle Paul tells us of Jesus' last words before He ascended to His Father:

> [4] And while staying with them he ordered them not to depart from Jerusalem, but to wait for the promise of the Father, which, he said, "you heard from me; [5] for John baptized with water, but you will be baptized with the

Holy Spirit not many days from now." Acts 1:4-5

I urge you to recognize your desperate need for the baptism in the Holy Spirit. I understand the apprehension; I understand the errant dogma; I understand the uncertainty, but the Word of God is so clear on the topic... the ministry of the Holy Spirit is *right now.* It is for *you.* His power is crucial for you to effectively present your work rendered of gold, and not stubble (1 Corinthians 3:12).

Please pray this prayer with me and take hold of the baptism in the Holy Spirit:

> Father, I completely submit my heart to You. I confess that I have neglected the baptism of the Holy Spirit and I repent before You today. I give You complete control, and I surrender all to You. I believe You want me to be filled to overflowing with your precious Holy Spirit, and I deeply desire to be baptized with the fire and power of Your Holy Spirit. Right now, I receive this baptism. Fill me Holy Spirit and take the lead in my life from this day forward. I surrender to You my spirit, mind, and body. Fill me to overflowing right now. In Jesus' name I pray. Amen.

My Closing Prayer

Lord, my personal prayer is that this work of Your hand will find its way into the heart of everyone whose lives and ministry you wish to empower through the baptism of Your sweet Spirit. Amen and amen.

Endnotes

1 Canfield, Jeff. The Promise of the Father. CreateSpace Independent Publishing Platform, 2015.

2 Cymbala, Jim. Fresh Wind, Fresh Fire. Grand Rapids: Zondervan, 1997.

3 Hohensee, Donald, and Allen Odell. Your Spiritual Gifts. Victor Books, 1992.

4 Drain, Wayne and Tom Lane. He Still Speaks. Southlake: Gateway Create, 2012.

5 Silk, Danny. Culture of Honor. Buchanan, NY: Destiny Image, 2013.

6 Green, Matthew D. Understanding the Fivefold Ministry. Lake Mary: Charisma House, 2005.

7 Scanlon, Paul. Crossing Over: Getting to the Best Life Yet. Nashville: Thomas Nelson, 2006.

8 Tubbs, Mark. Relational Transformation. Ascribe Publishing, 2017.

9 Dr. Jeff Canfield, The Promise of the Father: The Baptism of the Holy Spirit, (Self-published, 2015) p.103. (Note: Although there are points in the book with which I do not agree, with this one I most certainly do.)

10 Cessationism is a doctrine claiming that spiritual gifts such as the baptism in the Holy Spirit with the evidence of speaking in other tongues, prophecy, and healing ceased when Christ's early-church apostles died.

11 Vine, W.E., Vine's Complete Expository Dictionary of Old and New Testament Words. Nashville, TN: Thomas Nelson, 1996—38153rd edition.

12 Strong, James. New Strong's Exhaustive Concordance. Nashville, TN: Thomas Nelson, 2003— Super Value Series edition.

13 Liddel, Henry George, Henry Stuart Jones, Robert Scott, and Rob-

ert Mckensie. A Greek-English Lexicon. New York: Clarendon Press, 1940.

14 Tubbs, Mark. Relational Transformation. Ascribe Publishing, 2017.

15 Vine, W.E., Vine's Complete Expository Dictionary of Old and New Testament Words. Nashville, TN: Thomas Nelson, 1996—38153rd edition.

16 Strong, James. New Strong's Exhaustive Concordance. Nashville, TN: Thomas Nelson, 2003— Super Value Series edition.

CPSIA information can be obtained
at www.ICGtesting.com
Printed in the USA
BVHW030309110921
616282BV00004B/16